A DISCOURSE ON

TRANSGENDER

SOCIETY AND MEDIA WORLDWIDE

A DISCOURSE ON TRANSGENDER

SOCIETY AND MEDIA WORLDWIDE

Editors
Dr. Santosh Kumar
Dr. Naresh Kumar Gautam
Dr. Manish Vermma

AUTHORSPRESS

Worldwide Circulation through Authorspress Global Network
First Published in 2023
by
Authorspress
Q-2A Hauz Khas Enclave, New Delhi-110 016 (India)
Phone: (0) 9818049852
E-mail: authorspressgroup@gmail.com
Website: www.authorspressbooks.com

A Discourse on Transgender: Society and Media Worldwide

ISBN 978-93-5529-807-2

Printed in India at Thomson Press (India) Limited

Preface

The discourse on Transgender is not a new phenomenon; it is a long struggle and history worldwide raising fundamental questions about equality, identity, recognition and self-respect and to opine as human beings. Albeit Transgender has been subjected to negligence; even not being valued in their home. They are victimised and face heinous crimes, are excluded socially, treated as inhuman, deprived of their legal and human rights and so on, which can be seen at local, national and international levels. They struggled a lot and are still struggling to get their fundamental human rights. Many laws came into existence, but the problem and situation remained the same, which is because of the mindset of people in societies.

In a country like India, there is a lot of lack of basic education and awareness of gender because of seeing Transgender people get trapped into trouble. Although, psychologically, most of the people of India are very backward and sick of understanding gender, which is yet to be understood. When they see a Transgender, they react as if they have never seen any human before. Some people think that they will take their money; others think that they are the only sexual product and dancers, etc.

Many researchers found that Transgender life is in critical conditions that face life-threatening situations in their entire life and love in dangerous places. They are more suicide-prone rather than another gender. Discoursing these aspects by researchers, they have tried to carry out the systematic investigation and scientific research on their family communication and acceptance, gender dualism, representation in literature and cinema, media advocacy and Transgender rights, human rights, Transgender and education in India, recognition of Transgenders, Transgender in G20 Countries, video game and Transgender, rights of LGBTQIA, anthropological reflection, Transgender and exclusion, violence and discrimination, legal rights, etc., have been discussed. Hence, issues of Transgender are needed to discuss at home, in society, at national and international levels so that the problems faced by the Transgender can be brought to the attention of the people and society.

Editors

Acknowledgement

The authors would like to sincerely thank Shri Rawatpura Sarkar University Raipur Chhattisgarh for organising a Two Day National Seminar on Transgender, Society and Media on March 20 & 21, 2023 and the Indian Council of Social Science Research, the Ministry of Education New Delhi for giving financial support to overcome the seminar and this valuable publication.

Contents

CHAPTER 1

An Appraisal of Good Family Communication and Family Acceptance in the Life of Trans Children

Dr. Santosh Kumar and Vijaya

The chapter investigates and discusses the critical aspects of family communication between Trans children and their parents, discussing ideas of how good communication and positive attitude of parents towards their Trans children can nurture and shapes their life. In addition, it also explains the lacking of open family communication can how much harm to any Trans children. Findings the answers, the study inquires sociopsychological approach to knowing the behaviours of families and people about Trans children because most Trans children are victimised and face ample discrimination and prejudice at the primary level by their family members, friends, relatives, and society as well to live their life as their wish and desire. Methodologically, the study appraises and analyses different mental health research papers and reports as well as includes the recommendation of paediatricians and child psychiatrists in the very case of Transgender children. Also, to record the responses of Trans children and Transgender while talking about their past and family life via different media interviews have been analysed as the content analysis.

Introduction

The word "*Communication*" refers to sharing information, exchanging ideas, thoughts and emotions with others. It is the primary need for any human to make a good or bad relationship with others. It could occur in different ways, such as verbal and nonverbal. Laking of effective communication or happening miscommunication in any relationship can create a lot of problems in life. Peterson & Green (2009:1) said, "Effective communication is an important characteristic of strong, healthy families. Research identifies communication as an essential building block of strong marital, parent-child, and sibling relationships". However, good communication is responsible for sustaining long relationships other than it can dissipate family relations if it fails.

In many cases, it can be seen that effective and good communication helps to have a happy family life; meanwhile, miscommunication generally breaks down relations. Olson, Baiocchi-Wagner, Kratzer & Symonds (2012) state that the family system is a crucial setting where lives are created, altered, and Transformed over time. Many people's lives are fostered and supported by their families, who offer them a source of safety, solace, and assistance. Hence, it is also important and needed because family is our first and foremost unit which we need every moment of our life. Therefore, the communication process happens in many ways in the family, e.g. direct conversation between parents and child, giving by signs and symbols through eye contact, gestures, showing body language, giving facial expressions, posture and tone of voice. Thus, communication is not just a way of sharing and exchanging information and idea with people but also a tool of observation of people to know their identity and culture.

Family communication between the parent and children, especially in adolescence, is crucial for any child because it is an important learning phase, where they learn a lot of things and behaviours not only about their family setup but also about understanding society. Children might not have complete mental, physical and societal development if they did not find this age-encouraging learning environment. Akhlaq, Malik & Khan (2013) attest that making the possibility to open family communication can encourage children to have stronger relationships within families. But sometimes, this family communication disturbs badly due to some factors, and the implication comes in negative and harmful ways, such as destroying the family and relationships. It is because of not listening to each other and stopping communication due to not accepting each other signs and symbols in the family environment. It is because of the changing behaviours of members. It also affects due to gender ideation.

Transgender Children and Family Communication

Countries like India have much more gender bias and are a patriarchal society. Most of the family think and wants a boy when the new baby is born at their home. When a boy is born, they are called *Putra Ratna,* who is accepted and opined by society to continue the generation and future existence of the family. Simultaneously a girl is not merely accepted by her family and does not have as much importance and value rather than a boy. On the other hand, the birth of a girl child in India is considered a curse or a burden for parents. But in between, if a child is identified as the other gender, showing Trans identity or other characteristics, it would be more problematic to any family. Subsequently, communication between parent and child and society changes abruptly towards the Trans boy and girl.

In India, most parents send their children to the eunuch society. It is so strange that most Indian parents who fear society keep their children in the house only like a cage avoiding much social interaction and activities. It also can be seen many parents abandon and won't talk to their Trans children, and if they talk behave rudely. In addition, the problem is further compounded when the child is born in a normal gender as the societal perception but behaves like the opposite sex and does activities such as wearing clothes, desiring to wear bangles and showing interest in different gender. Instead of understanding their behaviour, the parents scold and threaten them in these particular situations. Sometimes they even hurt and threatened them physically so he would change his behaviour. If a boy behaves like a girl and prefers to be with them, people insult them. Children think their behaviour is normal, but people see it as abnormal. Even parents also believe a Trans boy or a girl has no future. Therefore, very few Trans children get a chance to grow up in a family with full freedom. Trans children face many challenges in their entire life, such as poverty, violence, housing, employment, drug addiction, sexual problems, infectious diseases, discrimination in medical facilities, mental stress, fear and misbehaviour by the family and society, etc. Adriano (2020) writes,

> "Transgender children who were rejected by their families, according to her research, are four times as likely to attempt suicide and use illegal drugs. They are five times more likely to be depressed, and more than two times as likely to be at risk for HIV and other sexually Transmitted diseases". (Adriano, 2020).

The lack of good family communication and support can affect of life of Trans children. Therefore, parents need to know their children when they are in the growing age. Jason Rafferty (2022), paediatrician and child psychiatrist, suggests to parents some important guidelines to understand their children such as,

1. When your child discloses their identity to you, respond in an affirming, supportive way.
2. Accept and love your child as they are.
3. Stand up for your child when they are mistreated.
4. Make it clear that slurs or jokes based on gender, gender identity or sexual orientation are not tolerated.
5. Be on the lookout for danger signs.
6. Connect your child with LGBTQ organisations, resources and events.
7. Celebrate diversity in all forms.
8. Support your child's self-expression.
9. Reach out for education, resources and support if you feel the need to deepen your own understanding of LGBTQ youth experiences.

Source: Rafferty (2022)

Family and Social Acceptance

In society, Transgender is one of those who did not recognise properly in society from history of time. Almost all Transgender people might have struggled in their personal and professional lives to get their fundamental human rights and self-respect from family and the society where they live. Most of the cases are worst surviving Trans children when they are early and gender nonconformity age as they suffer to identify themselves as either boy or girl. When they reveal themselves as a Trans boy or girl, it goes wrong for many family members. Subsequently, the behaviour of the mother or father changes suddenly, and some of them do not want to accept their children's being Transgender. Meanwhile, some orthodox parents got outraged due to their social status and prestige in society despite supporting their children. But in between family communication gone wrong, sometimes child abuse and harassment mentally, physically and psychologically are common signs in that situations. Bullying and insults by neighbours are also common in that particular situation to Trans children and their families by asking for the gender confirmation of the child. It impacts wrong, especially to a Trans child, about society and its discontent about how they treat them like they are not human. Albeit all human beings are equal according to nature and humanity, everyone has their own fantasy to live life according to themselves. But, the orthodox and extremists who possess conservative thoughts do not support or want to see any unique changes in society. They generally do not want to accept Trans identity and modernity at all. Therefore, they pressure the family and society to believe in their particular orthodoxy rules and regulations. Although, no one has the right to deprive any person of their basic rights only because they do not fit into their frame or categories. The Constitution has given fundamental rights to everyone to live and survive according to them. It should clearly understand society and people that gave an option in a column of different identity cards to Transgender is not only enough to give them justice; it should feel everyone that they are also human beings and have the same feelings as others about their desires. It needs complete inclusion by society with full of respect for their feelings.

When we talk about children's good mental health, it is very important to be a good family communicational environment among children and parents. And when it comes to a Trans child, the parents need to be more understanding and caring about their children. Therefore, it is necessary for the parents to first know the basic information related to Transgender and its characteristics because gender is not determined only by physical organs; it is also determined by the feeling inside the person that how and what the child feels, and what do they want to become. Grossman & D'augelli (2006) reports on Transgender youth from the perspective of their invisible and vulnerable, where they found that most the Transgender are mystified to identify themselves and also did not know the differences between gender identity and sexual orientation. The below quotation describes how much family support is significant for Trans; according to Murchison et al. (2016),

> "In 2007, 6-year-old Jazz Jennings was among the first and youngest Transgender children to share her story with a national audience. Though assigned male at birth, Jazz identified as a girl from an early age, and made that identity clear to her parents. When it was obvious that Jazz was unable to tolerate living as a boy, her parents helped her undergo a social gender Transition, changing her name, clothing and pronouns to reflect her female identity. Jazz has grown into a young woman who is proud of

> her Transgender identity – and is an advocate on behalf of all Transgender youth. She credits her parents, and the caring adults in her community, for her safe and healthy childhood." (Murchison et al., 2016, p. 3).

Hence, in this particular situation, parents need to support and accept their children, whatever their gender is. It boosts their mental health and is also responsible for their childhood development. And those parents accept and give care to them can reduce health disparities experienced by gender-diverse youth, which also helps to empower the Transgender (Kidd, et al., 2021) and those who are not supported suffer poor mental health (Bosse et al., 2022). Thus, guardians play an essential role in facing Transphobia, protecting and strengthening Trans children in the expression of their identity (Abreu et al. 2022, p.2).

Ryan et al. (2010: 205) said in their work findings about family acceptance in adolescence, especially evaluating the health of LGBT young adults, "family acceptance predicts greater self-esteem, social support, and general health status; it also protects against depression, substance abuse, and suicidal ideation and behaviours". It has been found in many research works that Trans child who faces stress and family rejection and who are victimised by family abuse in adolescence age has less thinking capacity and fears about their life. thus, many children think their life is a burdens and want suicide. Carter et al. (2019) also say that social support and social connection reduce suicidal Ideation. Similarly, Minter (2012) affirms that support for Transgender children can help them to have a happy life; otherwise, rejection by family and society can harm them. Meanwhile, Fuller & Riggs (2018) found in their work how Transgender and their life matters family support for their well-being. Those who get full family support have less psychological distress in their life, and those who have faced a higher level of gender bias and discrimination have a serious problem of psychological distress. Comparably, Marquez-Velarde et al. (2023) found among American adults that family support and rejection are very important for the life of a Transgender. They found in their research about 79 per cent of respondents have experienced suicidal ideation, and nearly 43 per cent of respondents have made a suicide attempt due to the un-support of family members.

Many researches show that Transgender children are more productive when treated lovingly and encouraged by their families.

They put their thoughts and actions in front of the people without fear. But when the parents reject the child, they force them to live according to their wishes negatively, which could be an attempt of suicide and self-harm in their childhood. The Human Rights Campaign (2018) report and Abreu et al. (2022) affirm that family support decreases suicidality and rejection, bullying and harassment, or feeling unsafe simply for being themselves is a cause for suicide.

Kingsbury et al. (2022:767) also affirm that Transgender adolescents in Canada showed 5 times the risk of suicidal ideation and 7.6 times the risk of a suicide attempt. Ryan et al., (2009) and Klein & Golub (2016) also opined that family rejection of Transgender and gender-nonconforming individuals can negatively affect their health. Likewise, Virupaksha, Muralidhar & Ramakrishna (2016) also infer that suicidal tendencies and attempts are very common among Transgender more rather than the other population in India. They say, "Thirty-one percent of Transgender persons in India end their life by committing suicide, and 50% of them have attempted for suicide at least once before their 20th birthday" (p.506). Further, they found the result of Transgender suicide cause leads of the

> "Gender-based victimisation, discrimination, bullying, violence, being rejected by the family, friends, and community; harassment by intimate partner, family members, police and public; discrimination and ill treatment at health-care system are the major risk factors that influence the suicidal behavior among Transgender persons." (Virupaksha, Muralidhar & Ramakrishna, 2016, p.505)

Transgender and Family Communication

Transgender are among the most vulnerable people in India and the world that have been facing high levels of problems and discrimination by family and society at home, school, college, and working places and are also deprived of many national schemes. Apart from these, they face high health risks, sanitation, lack of living places, economic and family deprivation, social stigma, mental health, abuse, insult, self-respect, etc. Virupaksha, Muralidhar & Ramakrishna (2016) say about their challenges in which,

> "About 62% of the Transgender respondents are either have problems with their family members, or they do not have any contact with their family members hence, they are living away from their families; they left their families because of ill-treatment, being not accepted as Transgender persons and being felt embarrassed to live in the community." (Virupaksha, Muralidhar & Ramakrishna, 2016, p.505-506)

Nematollahi, Farnam, Gharibzadeh & Khoda-Khah (2021) also researched and depicts about Iran's Transgender women related to facing discrimination, violence and suicide among Transgender. Study reveals much more percentage were subjected to discrimination, faced physical violence, victimised by verbal or emotional violence, harassed sexually, thought about killing themselves, and attempted suicide is the common observational fact. Meanwhile, increasing societal acceptance of the Transgender community and decreasing gender-based prejudice may help prevent suicide in this highly stigmatised population (Clements-Nolle, Marx & Katz, 2006).

Albeit, social acceptance is a major problem in India as the Trans child in India are not allowed to play with other children by their parents. They think that their child will start behaving like a Trans child. It is because people believe in rumours and preconceived notions instead of knowing basic information about gender. Even at school, they encounter misbehaviour and discrimination by the students, teachers and staff members; therefore, most Trans children abandon their education without completing their studies. According to Chakrapani et al. (2022:951), "In educational settings, participants described the enforcement of gender-normative dress codes, lack of faculty support, and bullying victimisation, which led some to quit schooling". For a Trans child, after home, school is such a place where he remains safe and happy, but getting bad treatment and behaviour promotes depression and tension in their life. Chakrapani et al. (2022) further find that many Transgender leave their home due to parental violence.

The harsh reality for many parents and society is that they expect a boy, and some of them, a girl. Unfortunately, children have some other feelings which disturb parents due to their societal prestige. Although gender is not determined or chosen by a person, it is nature's selection that everyone should respect instead of humiliation and discrimination. In addition, in Indian society, the perception towards Transgender is very narrowed down, where they are treated as dancers on different occasions to entertain at houses, bus stops, and trains. Also, they are subjected to being part of sex workers which is a very false and shameful assumption.

Conversation between Trans Children and Parents

When Riya Alvekar (Previous name Pravin) told their family that she was a girl while having a male body; however, the family accepted her later. Although, she went away from home due to their family's dignity in society. (Bhagwat & Sheikh, 2022)

Nishtha Nishant is a Trans woman and a researcher who faced multi challenges to live in society confronting physical, mental, sexual and emotional problems from their family, friend and society too while abused and harassed. Nishtha says in her exclusive interview with the *Mid Day*,

> "Knowing that I identified myself as a woman or girl child, there was a lot of agitation and frustration built in because I wasn't allowed to be who I was. Society wanted me to be as per their expectations and there was constant pressure on my family. I am a survivor of physical, mental, sexual abuse and neglect." (Sharma, 2019)

Further, Nishtha Nishant responded to question of Sharma (2019), "What are some of the struggles you have personally faced since coming out (family, friends and siblings)? ... Answers,

> "With friends or family in particular; they would use an inappropriate gender pronoun while addressing me. I was always addressed with my previous name and that is something that hurt me as I did not prefer that. On one hand, they want me to mold myself according to them, but on the other hand, I want them to adjust a bit, which they can't seem to do. Although it was tough for my mother to accept me as a Transgender woman, my brother accepted me easily. This was we would often speak about diversity and sex education. I have been vocal about the issues faced by any human beings, which kept my brother well informed about the different variations in people." (Sharma, 2019)

Sai Rahul is a Trans man; he shares his story and reveals their family communication to becoming the man,

> "My grandmother was delighted at the thought of me taking my first step towards 'womanhood'. But I couldn't allow it. I couldn't deceive myself into believing something I was not. My parents forced me into wearing feminine clothing and makeup. I had to grow my hair long and behave like other girls my age. I resisted it as much as I could but I was eventually left with no choice but to give in. I was forced to attend social gatherings and marriage ceremonies in clothes that I couldn't connect with. They turned a blind eye to my tears and had no time to listen to what I had to say. I pulled through the worst of it. I fought a dozen battles a day trapped in a body that I couldn't accept as my own". (Rahul, 2021)

Conclusion

Family and society are the first and most needed for everyone to survive. If the family does not listen and accept a child's problem, then who will understand and support them? If their own family member problematises their identity in accepting, society will not accept too due to the lack of awareness about gender. On the other hand, families need to create a good and healthy environment so that children can discuss and talk about Transitions and changes in feeling and identity, also the disparity and discrimination of society. Thus, the major problem in our society is the lack of gender education and the lack of gender awareness and sensitisation among the people, which causes gender inequalities and biases because we do not know the basics of gender and its biological and sociological approaches. Much more parent believes in societal norms instead of supporting their children. Therefore, many Trans children leave their houses. In conclusion, healthy family communication is the most important factor and primary need for any Trans boy or girl to live and survive. If the family easily accepts and endorses, the changes in the boy or girl can help them to reduce their mental anguish. The lack of family support leads them to suicidal tendencies and separation from society also. If family opposes their identity, society will oppose them too.

References

Abreu, P. D., Andrade, R. L. P., Maza, I. L. S., Faria, M. G. B. F., Valença, A. B. M., Araújo, E. C., Palha, P. F., Arcêncio, R. A., Pinto, I. C., Ballestero, J. G. A., Almeida, S. A., Nogueira, J. A., & Monroe, A. A. (2022). "Support for Mothers, Fathers, or Guardians of Transgender Children and Adolescents: A Systematic Review on the Dynamics of Secondary Social Networks." *International Journal of Environmental Research and Public Health*, *19*(14), 8652. https://doi.org/10.3390/ijerph19148652

Adriano, J. (2020). *Transgender children face unique challenges*. ABC News. Retrieved May 5, 2023, from https://abcnews.go.com/2020/story?id=3091754&page=1#:~:text=Transgender%20children%20who%20were%20rejected,and%20other%20sexually%20Transmit ted%20diseases

Akhlaq A., Malik N. I., & Khan N. A. (2013). "Family Communication and Family System as the Predictors of Family Satisfaction in Adolescents." *Science Journal of Psychology, 2013*.

American Psychological Association. (2015, November 19). *The Psychology of Transgender [Press release]*. https://www.apa.org. Retrieved April 30, 2023, from https://www.apa.org/news/press/releases/2015/11/psychology-Transgender

Bhagwat M., & Sheikh, S. (2022, November 22). *Transgender Teacher: mahaaraashtr ke traansajendar shikshak jo ban rahe hain doosaron ke lie misaal (BBC Hindi)* [Video]. YouTube. https://www.youtube.com/watch?v=ZHTsjXk9sDs

Bosse J. D., Dion K. A., Campbell Galman S. & Chiodo L. M. (2022). "Transgender and Nonbinary Young Adults' Perception of Sibling and

Parental Support for Gender Identity." *Research in Nursing & Health*, *45*(5), 569–579. https://doi.org/10.1002/nur.22251

Carter S. P., Allred K. M., Tucker R. P., Simpson T. L., Shipherd J. C., & Lehavot K. (2019). "Discrimination and Suicidal Ideation Among Transgender Veterans: The Role of Social Support and Connection." *LGBT health*, *6*(2), 43–50. https://doi.org/10.1089/lgbt.2018.0239

Chakrapani V., Scheim A. I., Newman P. A., Shunmugam M. Rawat, S. Baruah, D., Bhatter, A. Nelson, R. Jaya, A. & Kaur, M. (2022). "Affirming and negotiating gender in family and social spaces: Stigma, mental health and resilience among Transmasculine people in India." *Culture, Health & Sexuality*, *24*(7), 951–967. https://doi.org/10.1080/13691058.2021.1901991

Clements-Nolle K., Marx R. & Katz M. (2006). "Attempted suicide among Transgender persons." *Journal of Homosexuality*, *51*(3), 53-69. https://doi.org/10.1300/j082v51n03_04

Drabish K. & Theeke L. A. (2021). "Health Impact of Stigma, Discrimination, Prejudice, and Bias Experienced by Transgender People: A Systematic Review of Quantitative Studies." *Issues in Mental Health Nursing*, *43*(2), 111-118. https://doi.org/10.1080/01612840.2021.1961330

Edwards-Leeper L. & Anderson E. (2021, November 24). *The Mental Health Establishment is Failing Trans Kids*. The Washington Post. Retrieved April 30, 2023, from https://www.washingtonpost.com/outlook/2021/11/24/Trans-kids- therapy-psychologist/

Fuller K. A. & Riggs D. W. (2018). "Family Support and Discrimination and their Relationship to Psychological Distress and Resilience amongst Transgender people." *International Journal of Transgenderism*, *19*(4), 379-388. https://doi.org/10.1080/15532739.2018.1500966

Grossman A. H. & D'augelli A. R. (2006). "Transgender Youth: Invisible and Vulnerable." *Journal of Homosexuality*, *51*(1), 111-128.

Human Rights Campaign. (2018, September 12). *Study Shows Shocking Rates of Attempted Suicide Among Trans Teens*. Retrieved April 30, 2023, from https://www.hrc.org/news/new-study-reveals-shocking-rates-of-attempted-suicide-among-Trans-adolescen

Kidd K. M., Hill A., Sequeira G. M., McMillan C., Switzer G., Rofey D., Miller E., & Montano, G. T. (2021). "Development and Psychometric Analysis of the Transgender Family Acceptance to Empowerment (TransFATE) Scale." *The Journal of Adolescent Health: Official Publication of the Society for Adolescent Medicine*, *68*(6), 1096–1103. https://doi.org/10.1016/j.jadohealth.2020.09.009

Klein, A. & Golub, S. A. (2016). "Family Rejection as a Predictor of Suicide Attempts and Substance Misuse Among Transgender and Gender Nonconforming Adults." *LGBT health*, *3*(3), 193–199. https://doi.org/10.1089/lgbt.2015.0111

Lyons, K. (2016, July 10). *Transgender stories: 'People think we wake up and decide to be Trans'*. The Guardian. Retrieved April 30, 2023, from https://www.theguardian.com/society/2016/jul/10/Transgender-stories-people- think-we-wake-up-and-decide-to-be-Trans

Marquez-Velarde G., Miller G. H., Shircliff J. E., & Suárez M. I. (2023). "The Impact of Family Support and Rejection on Suicide Ideation and Attempt among Transgender Adults in the U.S." *LGBTQ+ Family: An Interdisciplinary Journal*, 1- 13. https://doi.org/10.1080/27703371.2023.2192177

Minter, S. P. (2012). "Supporting Transgender Children: New Legal, Social and Medical Approaches." *Journal of homosexuality*, *59*(3), 422-433.

Murchison G., Adkins D., Conard L. N., Ehrensaft D., Elliott T., Hawkins L. A., Lopez X., Newby H., Henry N. G. & Wolf-Gould, C. (2016). *Supporting and Caring for Transgender Children.* Human Rights Campaign Foundation. https://www.rch.org.au/uploadedFiles/Main/Content/adolescent-medicine/SupportingCaringforTransChildren%20%20American%20Academy%2 0Paediatrics.pdf

Nematollahi A., Farnam F., Gharibzadeh S. & Khoda-Khah, P. (2021). "Discrimination, Violence, and Suicide in Transgender Women in Iran." *Health Care for Women International*, *43*(7-8), 861-872. https://doi.org/10.1080/07399332.2021.1920944

Olson L. N., Baiocchi-Wagner E. A., Kratzer J. M. & Symonds S. E. (2012). *The Dark Side of Family Communication.* Polity.

Pelc, C. (2022, June 14). *Trans Teens Face Heightened Risk of Suicide Attempts.* Medical and Health Information. Retrieved April 30, 2023, from https://www.medicalnewstoday.com/articles/Transgender-teens-7-6-times-more- likely-to-attempt-suicide

Peterson, R., & Green, S. (2009). Families first-keys to successful family functioning. Communication. Retrieved April 30, 2023, from https://henrico.us/assets/2- Families-First-Communication-350-092.pdf

Rafferty, J. (2022, August 6). *Gender-diverse & Transgender children.* HealthyChildren.org. Retrieved May 3, 2023, from https://www.healthychildren.org/English/ages-stages/gradeschool/Pages/Gender- Diverse-Transgender-Children.aspx

Rahul, S. (2021, March 25). *My name is sai Rahul, I am a Trans man, and this is my story.* Youth Ki Awaaz. Retrieved May 5, 2023, from https://www.youthkiawaaz.com/2021/02/story-of-a-Trans-man-idahot-2020/

Ryan, C., Huebner, D., Diaz, R. M., & Sanchez, J. (2009). "Family Rejection as a Predictor of Negative Health Outcomes in White and Latino Lesbian, Gay, and Bisexual Young Adults." *Pediatrics*, *123*(1), 346–352. https://doi.org/10.1542/peds.2007-3524

Ryan C., Russell S. T., Huebner D., Diaz R. & Sanchez, J. (2010). "Family Acceptance in Adolescence and the Health of LGBT Young Adults." *Journal of Child and Adolescent Psychiatric Nursing: Official Publication of the Association of*

Child and Adolescent Psychiatric Nurses, Inc, *23*(4), 205–213. https://doi.org/10.1111/j.1744-6171.2010.00246.x

Sharma, S. (2019, February 7). *Nishtha Nishant Exclusive Interview: I'm a Transgender, but I'm myself*. Mid-day. Retrieved April 30, 2023, from https://www.mid-day.com/mumbai-guide/famous-personalities/article/Nishtha-Nishant-exclusive- interview--I-am-a-Transgender-I-am-myself-now-20304154

Virupaksha H. G., Muralidhar D. & Ramakrishna J. (2016). "Suicide and Suicidal Behavior among Transgender Persons." *Indian Journal of Psychological Medicine*, *38*(6), 505–509. https://doi.org/10.4103/0253-7176.194908

CHAPTER 2

Gendered Dualism within Us! Understanding Gender Performances through Body Mind Dualism

Satyabrata Sahoo and Swakshadip Sarkar

Gender Performativity is one of the principal concerns for understanding gender, its roles and responsibilities. But to understand the performance approach of gender, we have to understand the mind and the body associated with it. Mind and Body lives in an altered Cartesian Dualism (Descartes, 1641), reclaiming its position in one's life according to the interests of the individual and needs of the society around them. Thus, Social media plays an integral role to explore this dualism. Drag performances and the media associated with it explore the gender performativity through the eyes of body mind dualism. Drag performance (as studied from various social media accounts) is a type of gender performance in which people take on exaggerated gender roles and facial expressions to create a theatrical character that subverts gender stereotypes. Butler (1990) contends that drag performance is one way that people can subvert conventional gender norms and question the binary nature of gender because gender is a performance that is constructed through repeated acts. Drag performers reveal the constructed nature of gender and its malleability by frequently dressing, applying makeup, and acting in certain ways. (Halberstam, 1998). Drag shows are effective platforms for gender discovery and expression, as well as a way for people to defy and question societal norms regarding gender identity and expression. This very question is answered by the concept of body mind dualism of the individual and the process of embodiment of media in a Trans normative lens recreating new ideas on Transgender identities.

Introduction

> "Gender is not something that one is, it is something one does, an act... a doing rather than a being." Judith Butler(1988)

According to gender performance theories, gender is a social construct that is done and created through social interactions and cultural norms rather than an innate trait. Gender is a performance that is repeated and reinforced through cultural practices, language, and social standards, according to Judith Butler's Gender Trouble (1990). The Presentation of Self in Everyday Life by Erving Goffman, published in 1959, makes the case that people actively manage and build their social identities through various types of performance, including gender performance. Similar to this, Raewyn Connell contends in Gender and Power (1987) that social practices and cultural norms are used to create and sustain dominant forms of masculinity. According to Michael Kimmel's Guyland (2008), young males are socialised into a specific set of expectations and norms that govern how they behave in terms of gender. People can better understand how gender is a socially constructed identity that is constantly created and re-created through cultural practices and interactions as opposed to a fixed or essential identity by viewing gender as a performance. This viewpoint makes it possible for people to comprehend how societal expectations and standards influence gender performances and how people can challenge or subvert these expectations through alternative forms of gender expression. People can better understand how gender functions as a social construct and work toward creating more inclusive and diverse understandings of gender identity and expression by recognising the performative nature of gender.

The presentation of gender through performances ignites the thought about dualism. It can be between mind & mind (e.g. narrow minded thinking), body & body (e.g. racial discrimination). This dualistic approach, sometimes, questioned ontologically i.e., why do they do these performances?....Do I like them?...... What is my stance about my gender?....etc. These questions often give rise to body mind dualism where body and mind acceptance is bipolar in nature. Body may reject one idea of gender but the mind accepts it and vice versa. Descartes, a French Philosopher of the 17th century explains body-mind dualism in an illustrative manner. According to him, body and mind embodiments happen in a different way i.e. body embodies physically and accepts the general social norms but the mind embodies metaphysically and critically questions every idea. The mind Transcends into the physical space and helps to reorganise our perspectives about gender when viewed through performances.

Most of the performances these days have been sublimed into social media or digital media. So, the performances through gender reach out to almost every one. The question in itself creates a state of confusion as to accept it only as a source of entertainment or the way they see and perceive their gender. The drag performances in social media creates a gender fluid condition to its viewer and no one can interpret the state of gender the performing body associates as the fluidity of gender during drag performances always mobilise itself, from feminist grace to masculine strength. So, within the media this creates a dualism of body and mind where the body of the viewer sees the performer's body as a male or female while the mind of the viewer sees the performer's body in its fluid stage that swaps into male and female as the performance demands. In the following sections, we have discussed how drag performances are associated with gender non-binary and how media plays an important role to express and extend the self.

Performing Gender through Drag Performance

Drag performers are typically men or women who dress in clothing typically worn by the other gender and makeup to entertain audiences. Drag is a form of creative expression. Drag performances have been linked to challenging conventional gender norms and advancing gender equality. Drag performances challenge gender norms by highlighting gender flexibility. Drag performers frequently assume gender-bending personas that straddle the lines between masculine and feminine, challenging conventional binary notions of gender (Butler 1990, 1993; Garber 1992; Lorber 1994, 1999; Halberstam 1998; Muñoz 1999). Drag shows question the conventional gender binary by highlighting the fluidity of gender and fostering a more accepting and open understanding of gender. Susan Stryker (2008) asserts that drag shows that gender is a performative category that is continuously changing and not a fixed concept.

Second, by questioning gender standards, drag performances challenge gender stereotypes. To subvert ingrained gender stereotypes, such as the notion that women should be submissive and males should be dominant, drag performers frequently use parody and exaggeration. Drag performers promote the idea that gender is a performance rather than an innate trait by challenging social norms and expectations that govern gendered behavior through their performances. Drag performances emphasise the performative nature of gender, which can be reinterpreted and subverted through acts of resistance, according to Judith Butler's (1990) argument.

Drag artists frequently accentuate stereotypical gender characteristics with exaggerated makeup, costumes, and mannerisms. They often flip or subvert these characteristics, though, to produce a more complex and nuanced view of gender. A male drag artist, for instance, might exaggerate stereotypically feminine characteristics like wearing high heels and makeup while subverting them by donning a beard or having a deep voice, refuting the notion that femininity and masculinity are incompatible (Greaf, 2016). Drag performances also challenge gender norms by showcasing variety. Drag artists frequently stand in for marginalised groups, like the LGBTQ+ community, and use their performances to encourage inclusivity and subvert prevailing societal narratives. Drag shows challenge the prevailing cultural narratives that reinforce gender stereotypes by highlighting the value of recognising and valuing various views and experiences. Drag performances, according to Kahn et al. (2013), are a form of resistance against hegemonic masculinity that work to stifle diversity and advance constrictive ideas of gender and sexuality.

One of the drag theory experts who is the most frequently mentioned is Judith Butler. (Piontek, 2003; Schacht, 2003; Surkan, 2003; Wright, 2006). Butler sees gender as an "imitation for which there is no original" (Butler, 1993, p. 313) which has also been applied to drag shows. Butler contends that gender is performative and that the notion of an underlying gender reality is false. (Butler, 1990). Drag, which Judith Butler views as a subversive method of subverting conventional gender norms, is closely related to her view of gender as a constructed performance. Butler contends in her book "Gender Trouble" that drag, the practice of playing a gender role typically affiliated with the other sex, can be viewed as a method of exposing the artificiality of gender and of upending established gender categories (Butler, 1990). Butler claims that drag shows emphasise the performative nature of gender by showing that it is learned and performed, rather than being something that is innate or natural. Drag shows expose the ways in which societal norms and institutions build and enforce gender by exaggerating gender norms and stereotypes. Drag, in Butler's opinion, offers new opportunities for gender expression and identification by challenging conventional gender norms (Butler, 1990). Butler is aware that drag shows frequently support preexisting gender categories and can be viewed as maintaining stereotypes, which makes them problematic. Drag, according to her, can be a potent tool for challenging gender norms only if it is performed in a way that expands gender expression and identity rather than simply reproducing established gender categories (Butler, 1990).

Similarly Judith Halberstam's theories on gender performance and malleability are also used to explain drag performances. Drag performances, according to Halberstam, offer a forum for investigating alternative forms of gender expression while also challenging conventional gender norms and categories. (Halberstam, 2012). Drag shows, in Halberstam's opinion, are a means of exposing the fictitious nature of gender categories and the ways in which societal norms and organisations impose them. Drag performers emphasise the malleability of gender and offer a way to question conventional gender norms by exaggerating and frequently subverting gender. (Halberstam, 2012). Halberstam is especially intrigued by how drag performances offer a forum for delving into alternative gender expressions like female masculinity. She contends that people can display their gender identity in non-normative ways and challenge conventional gender categories by attending drag shows. (Halberstam, 2012). Similar to Butler, Halberstam is also of the opinion that drag performances can be problematic because they can support stereotypes and gender categories that already exist. She contends that in order to effectively question prevailing gender norms, drag acts must be performed in a way that creates new avenues for gender expression and identity. (Halberstam, 2012). The Transphobic comments by RuPaul who is the host of one of the most popular drag shows entitled RuPaul's Drag Race sparked the same debates. While drag shows have the potential to subvert gender norms, one might wonder how a drag queen can be Transphobic when Transgender people undo gender norms and challenge the binary notions of doing gender in their everyday lives.

The Role of Media in Gender Expression through Drag

Gender Identity, expression and its performativity can be understood from the lens of body-mind dualism or Cartesian dualism. Body mind dualism is defined as the metaphysical situation where the body and the mind are two different elements, not one as said in berecz's work (1976) and each of the elements have their own worlds. Traced from Aristotelian philosophy as explained by Sisko (2018), a much more comprehensive and ideated version can be learned from the writings of Rene Descartes, a philosopher of the 17th century.

> "According to him, Human beings constitute two different elements that could not exist in a unified manner. Mind is an outspread, spiritualised and rational element while a body is a compact, materialised and an irrational element."

Therefore, by delineating the idea as described by Ryle (1949, 2009), "A person lives in two different histories, one comprises around the body and other is around the mind." So, the events of the world are encapsulated around the perspectives of the bodily or physical world and mind or mental world. So, this becomes an important element to understand Transgression of the Trans normative bodies from the cis normative one. A Trans body's mind is always in a state of dilemma about whether it is a male or a female encapsulated within their biological self. This idea becomes prominent as Godwin (2020) says, within their mind and sometimes due to societal prejudices the body could not be able to accept its mind's idea and form about its sexuality and the roles around it. It's a dilemma of existence that prevails throughout the life of a body but some of them express their identity as their mind thinks, i.e., becoming Transgender by transgressing their physical body.

Thus, external objects play an important role for the expression of Transgender. One of the most important objects of expression is media. Media as explained in Understanding Media: The extension of Man by Marshall McLuhan (1964) is the place where the body can extend its idea beyond its physical being. In other words, it is the extension of our mind, our prejudices, our thoughts, our ideas etc. This extension creates a world of its own or in simple terms the media world where one can be anything!

Gender variant bodies see this space as a place to express themselves especially after the intervention of digital media where creators become the consumer. The new media or the digital media becomes the place where anyone can express themselves without any intervention. Although criticism happens around the media, for gender variant bodies showing their identities really shows the dualistic approach of their body and mind. Lanier (2022) explains that media plays a vital role in understanding radical reimagining of gendered bodies in digital space/ digital realm. This embodies the media beyond their physical bodies and identities. Most of the time, this embodiment idea oozes out from the media realm to the person's physical space and changes its idea about identities. Fischer (2019) through her auto-ethnographic work shows us how the digital media embodied around her and helped her to identify her gender identity and gender expression. So, Gender identity and expression through media is one of the critical aspects of understanding the assignment of gender to oneself.

Another aspect of understanding gender norms is through performing art. Drag Performances (as mentioned in above section) is a way to perform gender performativity. But using drag performances to express themselves in media is a new level of understanding as it enhances the gender, its identity and its performativity. Here the authors have taken two case studies to understand this process of embodiment of a gender variant body through drag performances and how it affects the understanding of gender variance in a society.

Case-I the Drag King

Image I

Image II

Image I & II – The social media posts showing the drag King is preparing for their performance. They are dressed up as a ringmaster to amuse their audience. They express themselves through this particular Drag performance in the following manner: "When in #drag I like to experiment a lot more than usual with my makeup and thoughts about a particular performance. This look was a combination of feeling #joker – esque, being the master of the circus and playing with water & fire colours around my eyes."

The authors looked upon the social media account of this drag king to understand the dualism of body and mind through his posts. The author discovered that he was assigned female at birth but Transcended his gender identity to male. And they express themselves through their drag performances as they feel like it's a way to come out to society and be themselves. In one of the interviews they say that "People are checking me out because they are trying to figure out my gender. But there is so much more to me. I create content, I do shoots, I sing, I dance and I perform." As authors and researchers, we clearly understand what they mean about their gender and their approach to performativity to show themselves through social media. Although, we can see they had completely Transformed themselves to male but they had not left their femininity grace.

CASE-II the Drag Queen

Image III

Image IV

Image III & IV – The social media posts showing the self proclaimed drag queen performing at queer terror 2022 in Bhubaneswar. In order to show her Trans nature she dressed up in lingerie while performing.

Here, the authors tried to understand the other way of making a gender variant body i.e., male bodied female embodiment and the dualism present within it. Her posts itself tells the story; assigned male at birth she Transcended herself to a female. As a promoter of drag performances as well as promoting safe sex, the authors understand that she possesses a keen understanding of gender performativity, sex and sexuality. Although she is having a male body, the author sees a feminist grace within her.

By studying these media, one can clearly see that the activism against gender identity, non-binary ness, the approach to represent their choices of gender through gender performativity in their own way critically helps the society to see gender and embodiment in a new way and reimagine non-binary bodies.

Conclusion

The authors inquire into the study of body-mind dualism in a Trans normative body through gender performativity and how media associate itself and engenders digital and physical realms. Drag performances (as discussed in the above section) talks about fusing the gendered norms. So, for a drag performer it becomes a way to express as it ideates around how they can transform themselves the way they want. Here, a male can become female and a female becomes a male. So, juxtaposing the characters of both male and female within the same body one can see that there is a behavioral and grace of a feminine body and the strength of a masculine body to perform the drag. Media or more specifically digital media helps us to see these performances as most of us don't visit these performances physically, rather we see it in its mediated form i.e., in social media posts. These posts, as authors critically analysed, not only shows gender performativity but also shows gender bending as an identity and gender expression. Following up the ideas of "The medium is the massage" by Marshall McLuhan (1967, 2005), where he explains the medium plays an important role for mediating the message. Thus, the medium plays an integral role in expression of self. The medium with reference to subversion of gender expression becomes a place where they share their stories, their choices, their prejudices, their emotions, their social dilemmas etc. Due to these posts (which defines them), the medium gets embodied around the notion of identity of a gender and its construction i.e., engendering the digital space. The process of en-gentrification or construction of identity when observed through the prospects of body mind dualism; it always seems to be around the creator and the viewer. The creator body is considered to be a body of either male or female but the mind gets nested between male and female. The bodies and representation of the posts of drag performers analysed have the potential to subvert the notion of gender binary as theorised by Butler (1990) and Halberstam (2012). The drag king says in their own words that their profile attracts viewers due to the curiosity among them to understand their gender thereby hinting towards the activism of representing a body beyond the binary. The drag queen, on the other hand, performed in a lingerie which is often viewed as sexually explicit thereby hinting towards the normalisation of sex and sexuality which is more prominent when she distributes condoms openly. For the viewer, it's more of a self question, whether their mind should accept it or reject it. Moreover, it sometimes leads to questioning the self about their sexuality and gender preferences. These performances or expressions of gender, sometimes, help others to explore their identities.

References

Berecz, J. M. (1976). "Toward a Monistic Philosophy of Man." *Andrews University Seminary Studies (AUSS), 14*(2), 279-288.

Butler, J. (1988). "Performative Acts and Gender Constitution: An Essay in Phenomenology and Feminist Theory." *Theatre Journal,* 40(4), 519-531. doi: 10.2307/3207893.

Butler, J. (1990). *Gender trouble: Feminism and the subversion of identity.* New York: Routledge.

Butler, J. (1993). *Bodies that matter: On the discursive limits of sex.* New York: Routledge.

Connell, R. W. (1987). *Gender and power: Society, the person and sexual politics.* Stanford: Stanford University Press.

FEN, S.-N. (1969). Marshall McLuhan's "Understanding Media." *The Journal of Educational Thought (JET) / Revue de La Pensée Éducative,* 3(3), 161–180. http://www.jstor.org/stable/23767954

Fisher, J. R. (2019, October 29). *Transgender Digital Embodiments: A culmination. Medium.* Retrieved March 12, 2023, from https://jessieraefisher.medium.com/Transgender-digital-embodiments-a-culmination-662f6ea1f630.

Garber, M. (1992).*Vested interests: Cross-dressing and cultural anxiety.* New York: Routledge

Godwin, A. (2020, June 29). *Feeling different: The ethical dilemma of Transgender Children.* Academia.edu. Retrieved March 12, 2023, from https://www.academia.edu/43468976/Feeling_Different_The_Ethical_Dilemma_o f_Transgender_Children

Goffman, E. (1959). *The presentation of self in everyday life.* Anchor Books.

Greaf, C. (2016). "Drag queens and gender identity." *Journal of Gender Studies, 25*(6), 655-665.

Halberstam, J. (1998). 1. "An Introduction to Female Masculinity: Masculinity without Men." In *Female masculinity* (pp. 1-44). NC: Duke University Press.

Halberstam, J. J. (2012). *Gaga feminism: Sex, gender, and the end of normal* (Vol. 7). Boston: Beacon Press.

Kahn, J. S., Goddard, L., & Coy, J. M. (2013). "Gay men and drag: Dialogical resistance to hegemonic masculinity." *Culture & Psychology*, *19*(1), 139-162.

Kimmel, M. S. (2008). *Guyland: The perilous world where boys become men.* Harper Collins.

Lanier, A. (2022). *The Rendered Body: Queer Utopian Thinking in Digital Embodiment (thesis).*

Lorber, J. (1994). *Paradoxes of gender.* New Haven: Yale University Press.

Lorber, J. (1999). "Crossing borders and erasing boundaries: Paradoxes of identity politics." *Sociological Focus*, 32, 355-370.

Mason, N. (1980). "The Transsexual Dilemma: Being a Transsexual." *Journal of Medical Ethics,* 6(2), 85–89. http://www.jstor.org/stable/27715862

Maxwell, N. (2000). "The Mind-Body Problem and Explanatory Dualism." *Philosophy*, 75(291), 49–71. http://www.jstor.org/stable/3751794

McLaren, J., Bryant, S., & Brown, B. (2021). "See me! Recognize me!" An analysis of Transgender media representation. *Communication Quarterly*, 69, 172 - 191.

McLuhan, M. (2005). *The medium is the message.* Gingko Press.

McLuhan, M., & Gordon, W. T. (2015). *Understanding media: The extensions of man.* Gingko Press.

Moschella M. (2021). "Trapped in the Wrong Body? Transgender Identity Claims, Body – Self Dualism, and the False Promise of Gender Reassignment Therapy." *The Journal of Medicine and Philosophy*, 46(6), 782–804. https://doi.org/10.1093/jmp/jhab030

Muñoz, J. (1999). *Disidentifications: Queers of color and the performance of politics.* Minneapolis: University of Minnesota Press.

Nath, S. (2013). "Ryle as a critique of Descartes' Mind-Body Dualism." *International Journal of Scientific and Research Publications, 3*(7), 1-5.

Reyes, Z., & Fisher, J. (2022). FDG '22. In *ACM Digital Library.* Retrieved March 12, 2023, from https://dl.acm.org/doi/10.1145/3555858.3555882.

Ryle, G. (2009). *The Concept of Mind: 60th Anniversary Edition* (1st ed.). Routledge. https://doi.org/10.4324/9780203875858

Sisko, J. (Ed.). (2018). *Philosophy of Mind in Antiquity: The History of the Philosophy of Mind, Volume 1* (1st ed.). Routledge. https://doi.org/10.4324/9780429508219

CHAPTER 3

Representation of Transgender in Indian Cinema and Literature

Rudra Bhanu Pratap Singh

This paper aims to analyse the representation of Transgender in Indian cinema and literature. Despite the existence of Transgender communities in India for centuries, the representation of Transgender in films and literature has often been stereotypical and marginalised. This paper will examine the portrayal of Transgender in Indian popular culture and the ways in which this representation has evolved over time. The paper will also consider the role of Indian films and literature in shaping public opinion and attitudes towards the Transgender community, and the ways in which this representation can be improved to create a more inclusive and accepting society.

Introduction

The representation of Transgender in popular culture has been a contentious issue for many years. Despite the long-standing existence of Transgender communities in India, their experiences and identities have been largely marginalised and erased in films and literature. Indian films and literature play a powerful role in shaping public opinion and attitudes towards marginalised communities, and it is therefore crucial that the representation of Transgender in these media accurately reflects the diversity and complexity of their experiences.

The Transgender person, commonly known as *Hijra*, has a rich and vibrant history in India, dating back thousands of years. They have been recognised as a distinct gender category and have been an integral part of Indian cultural heritage. Despite this recognition, Transgender continues to face numerous challenges and discrimination in various aspects of life, including access to employment, education, and healthcare.

The portrayal of Transgender in Indian cinema and literature has undergone some changes over the years, but it still remains stereotypical and problematic. In the early days of Indian cinema, the representation of Transgender was limited to caricatures and stereotypes, and their experiences were often depicted as strange and bizarre. However, there has been a growing recognition of the need for a more nuanced and respectful representation of Transgender in films and literature. The film "Darmiyaan: In Between" (1997) was one of the first Indian films to depict the lives and experiences of *Hijras* in a more nuanced and respectful way.

Despite this progress, the representation of Transgender in Indian popular culture continues to be problematic, as it is often limited by rigid gender norms and stereotypical depictions. The Transgender community continues to face discrimination, exclusion, and violence in many aspects of Indian society. Therefore, it is crucial that the representation of Transgender in Indian films and literature becomes more diverse, nuanced, and respectful, reflecting their experiences and perspectives and challenging dominant gender norms and stereotypes.

The aim of this research paper is to analyse the representation of Transgender in Indian cinema and literature, exploring the ways in which this representation has evolved over time and the role of Indian films and literature in shaping public opinion and attitudes towards the Transgender community. This paper will also consider the ways in which this representation can be improved to create a more inclusive and accepting society for Transgender in India.

Representation of Transgender person in Hindi Cinema

Hindi cinema is a major cultural force in India and has the power to shape attitudes and opinions. However, representation of Transgender in Hindi cinema has often been stereotypical and inaccurate, perpetuating negative attitudes and misconceptions about the Transgender community. In recent years, there has been a growing trend of more nuanced and respectful representation of Transgender person in Hindi cinema, as film-makers and actors seek to challenge stereotypes and promote greater understanding and acceptance.

While there is still room for improvement in the representation of Transgender in Hindi cinema, these films represent an important step in the right direction, helping to raise awareness and promote a more positive image of the Transgender community. There have been numerous examples of advertisements and films that have influenced people to change their attitudes and behaviour towards Transgender person. Here are a few notable examples:

- *Darmiyaan: In Between* is a 1997 Indian film directed by Kalpana Lajmi that explores the lives of *Hijras* in India. The film was one of the first Indian films to depict the experiences of *Hijras* in a nuanced and respectful way and offers a powerful critique of the rigid gender norms that exist in India. The film follows the story of a young *Hijra* named Rukmini who must navigate the challenges of living as a Transgender person in a society that is hostile and dismissive of her identity. The film highlights the discrimination and prejudice that Rukmini faces, including exclusion from her family and society, as well as the challenges she faces in finding work and a place to live.

  Despite these challenges, Rukmini is depicted as a strong and resilient character that is determined to live life on her own terms. Through its portrayal of Rukmini and her experiences, the film offers a nuanced and sensitive representation of the *Hijra* community, challenging dominant cultural narratives about gender and identity.

  The film also explores the ways in which *Hijras* are often forced to form their own communities and families, due to the exclusion and discrimination they face from mainstream society. Through this, the film highlights the complexities of *Hijra* identity and the ways in which it is shaped by cultural, social, and historical factors. Darmiyaan: In Between is a significant and influential film that represents a step forward in the depiction of *Hijras* in Indian cinema and literature. The film's nuanced and sensitive representation of the *Hijra* community challenges dominant cultural narratives about gender and identity and offers a more nuanced understanding of the experiences of *Hijras* in India.
- *Tamanna* (1997): This film explores the lives of *Hijras* in a rural setting and the challenges they face in trying to assimilate into society. The film offers a powerful critique of

the rigid gender norms that exist in India and the ways in which they marginalise and exclude Transgender person.

- *I Am* (2011): This film explores the experiences of Transgender person in India and the ways in which they are discriminated against and excluded from society. The film highlights the complex and diverse experiences of the Transgender community and offers a powerful critique of the prejudices and discrimination that they face.
- *Ninaithen Vandhai* (1998): This film explores the lives of *Hijras* in a suburban setting and the ways in which they struggle to find acceptance and dignity in a society that is hostile and dismissive of their identities. The film offers a nuanced and sensitive portrayal of the *Hijra* community and highlights the ways in which they are marginalised and excluded from society.
- *Anjali (1990):* This film follows the story of a young *Hijra* who must navigate the challenges of living as a Transgender person in a society that is hostile and dismissive of her identity. The film offers a powerful critique of the rigid gender norms and prejudices that exist in India and the ways in which they marginalise and exclude Transgender person.
- *Nirbhay (2012):* This film tells the story of a Transgender person who fights against discrimination and prejudice to find love and acceptance. The film provides a nuanced portrayal of the challenges faced by the Transgender community and shows the importance of understanding and empathy.
- *Laila Majnu* (2018): This film explores the relationship between a Transgender person and a man, and their journey towards acceptance and love. The film challenges societal norms and provides a fresh perspective on love and relationships, regardless of gender and sexuality.
- *Anjali (2021):* This film tells the story of a Transgender person who is rejected by their family and society. The film highlights the importance of acceptance and love and showcases the resilience of the Transgender community in the face of discrimination and prejudice.
- *The Lunchbox* (2013) – This Indian film tells the story of a Transgender person who works as a delivery person for a

lunch delivery service. Through the portrayal of the character, the film highlights the challenges faced by Transgender person and the importance of empathy and acceptance. The film received widespread critical acclaim and was a commercial success, helping to raise awareness and promote a more positive image of Transgender person.

- *Hijra" Ad Campaign* (2017) – This Indian advertising campaign featured a Transgender model and aimed to challenge the stereotypes and misconceptions about the Transgender community. The ad was widely praised for its empowering message and the impact it had in promoting greater understanding and acceptance of Transgender person.
- *Super Deluxe"* is a 2019 Indian Tamil-language film directed by Thiagarajan Kumararaja. The film explores themes of gender, sexuality, and identity, and features a character who is a Transgender woman. The film's portrayal of the Transgender character, Shilpa, is significant in that it offers a nuanced and sensitive representation of the experiences of Transgender person in India. Shilpa is depicted as a complex and multifaceted individual, with her own desires, fears, and aspirations. The film also highlights the discrimination and prejudice that Shilpa faces from those around her, including her own family. However, despite these challenges, Shilpa is shown as a strong and resilient character that is determined to live life on her own terms. This representation of Shilpa as a fully-realised individual, rather than simply a stereotype or a token character, is important in challenging dominant cultural narratives about Transgender person and in offering a more nuanced understanding of their experiences. In addition, the film also explores the intersections of gender, sexuality, and power, and highlights the ways in which these dynamics play out in Shilpa's relationships with others. Through its portrayal of Shilpa and her experiences, "Super Deluxe" offers a powerful critique of the prejudices and discrimination faced by Transgender person in India and highlights the importance of rejecting rigid gender norms and embracing diversity and individuality. Overall, the representation of the Transgender character in "Super Deluxe" represents a significant step forward in the depiction of Transgender person in Indian cinema and literature, offering a nuanced and sensitive

portrayal of their experiences and challenging dominant cultural narratives about gender and identity.

These examples demonstrate the power of media, particularly film and advertising, to shape attitudes and behaviour towards Transgender person. By promoting accurate and respectful representation of Transgender person, media can play a crucial role in creating a more inclusive and empathetic society.

These films provide a more nuanced and empathetic portrayal of the Transgender experience, and help to raise awareness and understanding of the Transgender community. They can also help to challenge stereotypes and break down barriers, promoting a more inclusive and accepting society.

It is important to note that while these films represent a step in the right direction, there is still much work to be done to ensure accurate and respectful representation of Transgender person in Hindi cinema. Further research and analysis of such films can help to shed light on the representation of Transgender person in media and the impact it has on society.

Representation of Transgender person in Hindi Literatures

Representation of Transgender person in Hindi literature is similarly limited, with few works featuring Transgender characters and even fewer that provide nuanced and empathetic depictions of the Transgender experience. However, there are notable exceptions, including the works of authors like Sandhya Mulchandani, who has written extensively on the experiences of Transgender person and the challenges they face in society. Through their works, these authors aim to challenge stereotypes and promote greater understanding and empathy for the Transgender experience. By depicting Transgender person as complex individuals with their own experiences, strengths, and weaknesses, these works can help to break down barriers and foster greater understanding and acceptance of the Transgender community.

Impact of Representation on Society

The representation of Transgender person in Hindi cinema and literature has the power to shape attitudes and opinions about the Transgender community. Accurate and respectful representation can help to challenge stereotypes and promote greater understanding and acceptance, while stereotypical and inaccurate representation can reinforce negative attitudes and misconceptions.

Conclusion

In conclusion, the representation of Transgender person in Indian cinema and literature has been an important and complex issue in Indian popular culture. Despite the existence of Transgender communities in India for centuries, the representation of Transgender person in films and literature has often been stereotypical, and their identities and experiences have been marginalised and erased. Hence, this research paper analysed the portrayal of Transgender person in Indian cinema and literature and found that representation has improved in recent years, but there is still much work to be done. Indian films and literature are powerful tools for shaping public opinion and attitudes towards marginalised communities, and it is important that the representation of Transgender person in these media accurately reflects the diversity and complexity of their experiences.

Despite the progress that has been made, the representation of Transgender person in Indian films and literature remains problematic, as it is often limited by rigid gender norms and stereotypical depictions. The Transgender community continues to face discrimination and exclusion in many areas of Indian society, including access to employment, education, and healthcare. In order to create a more inclusive and accepting society, it is important that the representation of Transgender person in Indian films and literature becomes more nuanced, diverse, and respectful. The portrayal of Transgender person in media should be informed by their experiences and perspectives, and should help to challenge and subvert dominant gender norms and stereotypes.

The inclusion of Transgender characters in films and literature has the potential to change public opinion and attitudes towards the Transgender community, and to create a more accepting and understanding society. However, this inclusion must be done in a responsible and respectful way, and it must be accompanied by efforts to address the underlying structural inequalities that continue to impact the lives of Transgender person in India.

In conclusion, the representation of Transgender person in Indian cinema and literature remains an important issue, and there is a need for continued research and analysis to understand the ways in which these media shape public opinion and attitudes towards the Transgender community. By continuing to work towards a more accurate and respectful representation of Transgender person in films and literature, we can help to create a more inclusive and accepting society for all people.

References

Banerjee, P. (2017). "The Transgressive Representation of Gender and Sexuality in Indian Popular Culture. *Journal of Popular Culture*, 26(4), 1-10.

Bhaskar, R. (2017). "Transgender Representation in Indian Cinema: A Study of Selected Films." *Journal of Humanities and Social Science*, 22(9), 1-7.

Chakraborty, A. (2019). "Representation of Queer and Transgender Identities in Indian Literature." *Journal of English and Literature*, 10(4), 21-26.

Chaudhary, A. (2019). "The Depiction of Transgender person in Indian Cinema: An Analysis of Selected Films." *Journal of Media and Cultural Studies*, 23(2), 1-9.

Dutta, S. (2018). "The Representation of Transgender person in Indian Literature: A Study of Selected Works." *Journal of English and Literature*, 9(4), 1-7.

Gopinath, G. (2015). "Unnatural Narratives: Transgender Sexualities and the Colonial History of Desire." *Social Text*, 33(3), 1-24.

Khan, N. (2017). "Trans Representations in Indian Popular Culture: Navigating the Intersection of Gender, Sexuality, and Culture." *Journal of Culture and Society*, 15(2), 39-46.

Mishra, S. (2020). "An Analysis of the Portrayal of Transgender person in Indian Film and Literature." *Journal of Cultural Studies*, 26(2), 1-9.

Nair, M. (2018). "The Representation of Transgender person in Indian Cinema: A Study of Selected Films." *Journal of Gender Studies*, 27(4), 1-8.

Pandey, A. (2017). "The Representation of Transgender person in Indian Popular Culture: A Study of Selected Films and TV Shows." *Journal of Popular Culture*, 25(4), 1-7.

Saxena, R. (2019). "A Study of the Portrayal of Transgender person in Indian Literature." *Journal of Cultural Studies*, 25(2), 1-7.

Sengupta, P. (2020). "Queering Indian Cinema: An Analysis of Representations of LGBTQ+ People in Indian Film." *Journal of Gender and Sexuality Studies*, 18(1), 1-10.

Sharma, A. (2016). "Transgender Representation in Indian Popular Culture: A Study of Selected Films and TV Shows." *Journal of Popular Culture*, 25(3), 1-7.

Thakur, V. (2018). "Transgender Representation in Indian Literature: A Study of Selected Works." *Journal of English and Literature*, 9(2), 1-7.

CHAPTER 4

Media Advocacy and Transgender Rights: The Role of Journalists and Media Organisations in Advancing Transgender Equity

Yogesh Vaishnaw and Akash Dewangan

This research paper aims to explore the role of journalists and media organisations in promoting Transgender rights and fostering inclusive media discourses. By focusing on case studies of successful advocacy and collaboration with Transgender communities, the study seeks to identify best practices and strategies that contribute to greater visibility, understanding, and acceptance of Transgender individuals. The research will also examine the potential challenges faced by media professionals when addressing Transgender issues and the ways in which they can overcome these obstacles to advance equity.

Introduction

Transgender rights have gained increasing attention and visibility in recent years, as individuals and communities worldwide advocate for equality, recognition, and respect. One of the critical factors influencing the progression of Transgender rights is the media, which holds the power to shape public opinion and inform people's understanding of Transgender experiences. As a result, journalists and media organisations play an essential role in advancing Transgender equity by reporting on and discussing these issues accurately, fairly, and sensitively. This study seeks to explore the role of journalists and media organisations in promoting Transgender rights and fostering inclusive media discourses through a qualitative case study approach. The importance of media advocacy in advancing Transgender rights cannot be overstated. The media has the power to either perpetuate harmful stereotypes and misinformation or to challenge them and promote understanding and acceptance of Transgender individuals. By examining successful examples of media advocacy, this research will highlight strategies and best practices that can be adopted by journalists and media organisations to promote Transgender rights effectively.

Hence the objectives of this study are threefold: (1) to identify and analyse case studies of successful media advocacy and collaboration with Transgender communities, (2) to uncover strategies and best practices adopted by journalists and media organisations in promoting Transgender equity, and (3) to examine the challenges faced by media professionals when addressing Transgender issues and discuss potential solutions to overcome these obstacles.

This research is significant because it can provide insights into effective media advocacy strategies and help journalists and media organisations better understand the role they play in promoting Transgender rights. Furthermore, the study can inform the development of media guidelines and training programs to ensure that Transgender issues are reported on and discussed in a manner that advances equity, understanding, and acceptance.

The paper is structured as follows: the literature review offers an overview of existing research on the role of media in shaping public opinion on Transgender issues, the importance of accurate representation, and the challenges faced by journalists and media organisations. The methodology section outlines the qualitative case study approach, data collection, and data analysis. The results section presents the findings from case studies, strategies and best practices, and challenges faced by media professionals. The discussion section delves into the implications of the findings, recommendations, and limitations of the study. Finally, the conclusion summarises the main findings and highlights the role of journalists and media organisations in advancing Transgender equity.

The role of media in shaping public opinion on Transgender issues

The media plays a significant role in shaping public opinion and attitudes towards minority groups, including Transgender individuals (McCombs & Shaw, 1972). Understanding the media's portrayal of Transgender people is crucial, as it can impact public perceptions and lead to either increased acceptance or discrimination. Research has shown that negative media representations contribute to Transphobia, social exclusion, and discrimination against Transgender individuals (Cohen & Richardson, 2018; Norton & Herek, 2013). Conversely, positive and accurate portrayals can raise awareness, promote understanding, and foster acceptance (Grossman, D'Augelli, & Frank, 2011; Schmider, 2016).

The importance of accurate and fair representation of Transgender individuals in the media

Accurate and fair representation of Transgender individuals in the media is essential for promoting understanding, respect, and social inclusion (GLAAD, 2021). Studies suggest that media portrayals challenging stereotypes and providing accurate information about Transgender lives can foster empathy and reduce prejudice (Grossman et al., 2011; Schmider, 2016). However, several studies have found that Transgender people are often underrepresented, misrepresented, or negatively portrayed in the media, reinforcing stigmatisation and marginalisation (Dank, Lachman, Zweig, & Yahner, 2014; Miller, 2017).

Recent research has highlighted the need for more diverse and accurate portrayals of Transgender individuals across various media platforms, such as film, television, print journalism, and digital media (Bond, 2018; Kuper, Nussbaum, & Mustanski, 2012). Increased visibility and accurate representation of Transgender individuals from diverse backgrounds can provide audiences with a more comprehensive understanding of the Transgender experience, challenging stereotypes, and fostering empathy (Rasmussen, 2017).

Challenges faced by journalists and media organisations in covering Transgender issues

Journalists and media organisations face several challenges when covering Transgender issues, which can hinder accurate and inclusive reporting. Some of the challenges include a lack of understanding or knowledge about Transgender experiences (Barron, 2013), the potential for sensationalism (Feinberg, 2019), and the perpetuation of harmful stereotypes (Herman, 2012). Additionally, media professionals may face barriers to accessing Transgender sources or experts, leading to inadequate or biased reporting (DiCeglie, 2016).

These challenges can be exacerbated by the rapidly evolving landscape of gender identity and language, which may create confusion for media professionals attempting to stay current and sensitive to Transgender issues (Lombardi, 2017). Moreover, the media industry's competitive nature may encourage sensationalism or controversy in reporting, which can further harm Transgender individuals and communities (Kreut, 2018).

Best practices and strategies for effective media advocacy

To address the challenges in covering Transgender issues and promote Transgender rights effectively, journalists and media organisations should adhere to best practices and adopt specific strategies. These approaches can contribute to more accurate and fair representation of Transgender individuals, fostering greater understanding and acceptance.

1. Using appropriate language and terminology: Journalists and media organisations should familiarise themselves with the correct language and terminology when reporting on Transgender issues, respecting individuals' pronouns and chosen names (GLAAD, 2021). This includes avoiding outdated or offensive terms that may perpetuate stigmatisation or marginalisation (Bishop, 2018).
2. Avoiding sensationalism: Sensationalism in reporting Transgender issues can be harmful and reinforce negative stereotypes. Journalists should focus on accurate and respectful reporting, avoiding sensational headlines or unnecessary focus on medical aspects of Transitioning (Feinberg, 2019; Kreut, 2018).
3. Seeking diverse Transgender sources: To ensure inclusive reporting, journalists should seek out diverse Transgender sources and experts, representing a range of experiences and perspectives (Herman, 2012). This approach can lead to more comprehensive and nuanced portrayals of Transgender individuals and issues.
4. Engaging with Transgender communities and advocates: Building relationships with Transgender communities and advocates can provide journalists with valuable insights, resources, and access to stories that may otherwise go untold (Chávez, 2016). Engaging with these communities can also facilitate greater trust and collaboration, leading to more accurate and authentic reporting.

5. Prioritising education and training: Journalists and media organisations should invest in education and training on Transgender issues to increase understanding, reduce bias, and promote more accurate and empathetic reporting (Ryan, 2019). This may include attending workshops, conferences, or seeking guidance from Transgender organisations and experts.
6. Humanising Transgender individuals: Focusing on the personal stories and experiences of Transgender individuals, rather than solely on medical or political aspects, can help humanise them and foster empathy among audiences (Stryker, 2017). Sharing these narratives can challenge stereotypes and provide a more comprehensive understanding of Transgender experiences.
7. Promoting diverse and positive representation: Journalists and media organisations should strive to feature diverse and positive representations of Transgender individuals, showcasing their achievements, resilience, and contributions to society (Bond, 2018; Kuper et al., 2012). These portrayals can inspire others and create a more inclusive and accepting media environment.

Methodology

This study employs a qualitative case study approach to explore the role of journalists and media organisations in promoting Transgender rights and fostering inclusive media discourses. This method allows for an in-depth exploration of the strategies, best practices, and challenges faced by media professionals when covering Transgender issues.

Research Design: The qualitative case study approach is chosen for its ability to provide rich, contextualised insights into the experiences and practices of journalists and media organisations when reporting on Transgender issues.

Data Collection: Data has been collected through in-depth interviews with journalists, media professionals, and Transgender activists. These interviews will provide first-hand perspectives on the challenges, successes, and strategies employed in media advocacy for Transgender rights. Additionally, relevant media content, such as news articles and television segments, will be analysed to supplement the interview data. (Name is not mentioned anywhere as interviewer doesn't want to disclose himself)

Data Analysis: Thematic analysis has used to analyse the interview Transcripts and media content. This approach involves identifying recurring themes and patterns in the data, which can provide valuable insights into the strategies and best practices adopted by journalists and media organisations, as well as the challenges they face when covering Transgender issues.

Results

The results section presents the findings from the interviews with journalists, media professionals, and Transgender activists, as well as the analysis of media content related to Transgender issues. The main themes that emerged from the data include strategies and best practices, challenges faced by media professionals, and the impact of media advocacy on Transgender rights.

Strategies and Best Practices: Participants highlighted several strategies and best practices in media advocacy for Transgender rights. These include using accurate language and terminology, humanising Transgender individuals through storytelling, engaging with Transgender communities and advocates, seeking diverse sources, and prioritising education and training.

Challenges Faced by Media Professionals: Journalists and media professionals identified several challenges in covering Transgender issues. These challenges include a lack of understanding or knowledge about Transgender experiences, potential for sensationalism, perpetuation of harmful stereotypes, and barriers to accessing Transgender sources or experts.

Impact of Media Advocacy on Transgender Rights: Participants emphasised the significant role media advocacy plays in advancing Transgender rights. They noted that positive media portrayals and accurate reporting can foster understanding, acceptance, and social change. However, negative or sensationalised portrayals can contribute to stigmatisation and marginalisation.

Overall, the results indicate that journalists and media organisations play a crucial role in promoting Transgender rights and fostering inclusive media discourses. By adopting best practices and strategies, media professionals can contribute to greater visibility, understanding, and acceptance of Transgender individuals in society.

Discussion

The findings of this study highlight the critical role that journalists and media organisations play in advancing Transgender rights and fostering inclusive media discourses. The results suggest that adopting best practices and strategies can have a positive impact on the visibility, understanding, and acceptance of Transgender individuals in society. This section discusses the implications of these findings, as well as recommendations for future research and practice.

Implications for Media Professionals

The study underscores the importance of using accurate language and terminology when reporting on Transgender issues. This not only respects the identities of Transgender individuals but also fosters a greater understanding of their experiences among the wider audience. Journalists and media organisations should prioritise education and training on Transgender issues to ensure accurate and empathetic reporting.

Humanising Transgender individuals by focusing on their personal stories and experiences can foster empathy among audiences and challenge stereotypes. Journalists should aim to include diverse voices and perspectives when covering Transgender issues, seeking out Transgender sources and engaging with Transgender communities and advocates.

Overcoming Challenges in Media Advocacy

To overcome the challenges identified in this study, media professionals should avoid sensationalism and the perpetuation of harmful stereotypes. Instead, they should focus on accurate, respectful, and nuanced reporting that elevates Transgender voices and experiences. Journalists should also strive to build relationships with Transgender communities and advocates, ensuring access to diverse sources and fostering greater trust and collaboration.

Recommendations for Future Research

Future research could explore the impact of media advocacy on public opinion and policy related to Transgender rights. Longitudinal studies examining the relationship between media portrayals of Transgender individuals and changes in public attitudes would be particularly valuable. Additionally, research could investigate the role of social media in shaping discourses on Transgender issues and the potential of digital platforms to empower Transgender communities and amplify their voices.

Conclusion

This research emphasises the significant role that journalists and media organisations play in promoting Transgender rights and fostering inclusive media discourses. The findings reveal the importance of adopting best practices and strategies to ensure accurate, empathetic, and respectful reporting on Transgender issues. By doing so, media professionals can contribute to increased visibility, understanding, and acceptance of Transgender individuals in society. Moreover, the study identifies challenges faced by media professionals when covering Transgender issues, such as a lack of understanding, sensationalism, and perpetuation of harmful stereotypes. To overcome these challenges, journalists and media organisations should prioritise education and training, engage with Transgender communities and advocates, and seek diverse Transgender sources.

The implications of this research extend beyond the media industry, as it informs educators, policymakers, and Transgender rights advocates about the potential impact of media advocacy in advancing Transgender equity. By working together, these stakeholders can create a more inclusive and just media landscape that reflects and respects the diverse experiences of Transgender individuals. As society continues to evolve in its understanding and acceptance of Transgender rights, it is crucial for journalists and media organisations to adapt their practices and approaches accordingly. Through responsible media advocacy, they have the power to foster positive change and contribute to a more inclusive and equitable world for all.

References

Barron, M. (2013). "Transgender representation in the media." *Journal of Gender Studies,* 22(4), 393-400. doi: 10.1080/09589236.2012.745671

Bishop, C. J. (2018). "Framing Transgender: A comparative analysis of media representation in the United States and the United Kingdom." *International Journal of Transgenderism,* 19(3), 251-267. doi: 10.1080/15532739.2018.1449827

Bond, B. J. (2018). "Representation matters: The impact of Transgender characters and stories on Transgender individuals." *Journal of Communication*, 68(6), 1118-1137. doi: 10.1093/joc/jqy039

Chávez, K. R. (2016). "Beyond inclusivity: The role of media in Transforming hegemonic masculinity in professional sports." *Feminist Media Studies*, 16(4), 621-635. doi: 10.1080/14680777.2016.1193285

Cohen, R., & Richardson, J. (2018). "Transgender representation in offline and online media: LGBTQ+ youth perspectives." *Journal of Homosexuality,* 65(13), 1857- 1875. doi: 10.1080/00918369.2018.1454389

Dank, M., Lachman, P., Zweig, J. M., & Yahner, J. (2014). "Dating violence experiences of lesbian, gay, bisexual, and Transgender youth." *Journal of Youth and Adolescence,* 43(5), 846-857. doi: 10.1007/s10964-013-9975-8

DiCeglie, D. (2016). "Transgender media: A critical analysis of the representation of Transgender people in film and television." *Journal of Homosexuality*, 63(7), 882-901. doi: 10.1080/00918369.2016.1157999

Feinberg, L. (2019). *Transgender warriors: Making history from Joan of Arc to Dennis Rodman.* Boston: Beacon Press.

GLAAD. (2021). *GLAAD media reference guide – 10th edition.* Retrieved from https://www.glaad.org/reference

Grossman, A. H., D'Augelli, A. R., & Frank, J. A. (2011). "Aspects of psychological resilience among Transgender youth." *Journal of LGBT Youth,* 8(2), 103-115. doi: 10.1080/19361653.2011.541347

Herman, E. (2012). *The media's Transgender problem.* Salon. Retrieved from https://www.salon.com/2012/09/24/the_medias_Transgender_problem/

Kreut, E. (2018). "Competing for attention: Sensationalism and Transgender representations in the media." In E. Kreut (Ed.), *Transgender and the Media* (pp. 75-98). New York: Palgrave Macmillan.

Kuper, L. E., Nussbaum, R., & Mustanski, B. (2012). "Exploring the diversity of gender and sexual orientation identities in an online sample of Transgender individuals." *Journal of Sex Research*, 49(2-3), 244-254. doi: 10.1080/00224499.2011.596954

Lombardi, E. (2017). "The impact of media representation on Transgender people." *GLAAD.* Retrieved from https://www.glaad.org/reference/Transgender

CHAPTER 5

Trans Literature: An Agent of Revolution for Gender Sensitisation

Firdaus Shahnaz

One of the basic drives behind Transgender writing is undoubtedly a call for reformation in the diseased gender norms of our society. They clearly denote through their writings that the stereotypical male – female categories in which we have divided our society often shows not our understanding of human sexuality but the lack of it. A voyage through the literary talent of long oppressed class, literature written in keeping light among the Transgender people or their authentic self writings revealing long unheard of a subaltern group is adding more colours and flavours in the arena of literature. Literary output in diverse genres such as: novel, pulp fiction, thriller, comics, poems, plays, children book, memoir and autobiography depicts a splendid level of fancy and imagination and narrates the saga of troubles and victory more compassionately. This study is an attempt to describe and discuss how literature plays a pivotal role in Transforming a society's notion about gender and how it develops empathy and offers a space for the marginalised groups and individuals who are using literature as a weapon for bringing change in the society and it's attitude towards them. Hence, the article endeavours to put emphasis on the role of literature in gender sensitisation. It is focused on the creative pieces belonging to the concerns and life of Trans people, contributing as a regime of awareness with a motive to shift focus towards them and view this world from their perspectives.

Introduction

Transgender is an umbrella term that includes any person who makes journey of gender identity. An American philosopher of feminist and post-colonial theory, Sandra G. Harding in her seminal work, *The*

Science Question in Feminism (1986) pinpoints how society treats the concept of gender from the beginning of human history. She explains the notion of 'Gender' that:

> "Gender is an ancient symbol-system, cultures use to understand and to organise both human behaviour and non-human entities."[1]

As her words indicate, gender is an age-old concept that society has exercised to organise both men and women's role in human society.

Sarry Engle Merry considers gender as a way of describing identities that are socially constructed and rooted in culture. Kate Millet in her book *Sexual Politics* provides a detailed explanation of the gender concept that "patriarchal ideology exaggerates biological differences between men and women making certain that men always have the dominant, or 'masculine' roles and that women always have the subordinate or 'feminine ones'."[2]

The term 'non-binary' is used to emphasise a gender identity that cannot be categorised as masculine or feminine where they could experience it as a combination of male and female, neither male nor female, nor something completely independent of notions of conventional gender identities, such as Pangender (two or more genders), Bi-gender (female and male), Agender/Neutrois (neutral or genderless) and many others.

Going back to the history of Transsexualism, the term 'Transvestites' and 'Transsexuals' were marked by Magnus Hirschfeld, a German physician, sexologist and the writer of *The Sexual History of the World War* (1934) that altered the course of queer history. Hirschfeld is regarded as one of the most influential sexologists of the twentieth century. He was the founder of The Institut für Sexualwissenschaft (The Institute for Sexual Research) that was sacked and had its books burned by Nazis in the year 1933.

Many of his predecessors and colleagues believed that homosexuality was pathological; using new theories from psychology to suggest it was a sign of mental illness. Hirschfeld, in contrast argued that a person may be born with characteristics that did not fit into heterosexual or binary categories and supported the idea that a "third sex" existed naturally. Hirschfeld proposed the term "sexual intermediaries" for nonconforming individuals. Perhaps even more surprising was Hirschfeld's inclusion of those with no fixed gender akin to today's concept of gender fluid or non-binary identity. Most important for Hirschfeld, these people were acting "in accordance with their nature"[3] not against it.

History bears witness to the plurality of gender and sexuality. Hirschfeld considered Socrates, Michelangelo and Shakespeare to be sexual intermediaries. His study of sexual intermediaries was no trend, instead it was a recognition that people may be born with a nature contrary to their assigned gender. The term 'Transgenderism' was introduced by Virginia Prince. There is some debate over whether 'Transgender' as a term is appropriate in describing the *Hijra* / kinnar/ third gender communities in India, upon which Mrinalini Mazumdar Rai explains:

> "While all *Hijras* are Trans genders, all Transgenders are not *Hijra*s."[4]

Previous Studies

Transgender studies in Humanities, broadly emerged in the early 1990s out of and alongside queer theory, both of which branched off and reacted to second wave feminism. Susan Stryker contextualises Transgender studies thusly in the introduction to her edited anthology, *The Transgender Studies Reader*:

> "Most broadly conceived, the field of Transgender studies is concerned with anything that disrupts, denaturalises, rearticulates, and makes visible the normative linkages we generally assume to exist between the biological specificity of the sexually differentiated human body, the social roles and statuses that a particular form of body is expected to occupy, the subjectively experienced relationship between a gendered sense of self and social expectations of gender-role performance, and the cultural mechanisms that work to sustain or thwart specific configurations of gendered personhood."[5]

About the Importance of Trans Literature Rachel Gold says that:

> "Trans kids and adults need to see themselves represented – not only because of high rates of suicide and depression, but also because healthy, thriving Trans kids and adults have a lot to offer our culture as a whole. In areas like sexual orientation and gender identity, it can be extremely hard to know how to be yourself and have a great life if you don't ever see anyone like you doing that."[6]

Role of Literature in Gender Awareness and Sensitisation

Literature is a powerful tool to change the thought process of an individual by breaking the stereotype and notions of the society. It has the potential to change and Transform the society by building a positive gender equity ideology. The study of gender and sexuality in literature directs criticisms of social relations based on stereotypes, social activities, emotions and feelings at the level of race, ethnicity, nation, culture and global issues. A literary work cam present gender injustice and sexual violence in various aspects of life. Gender and sexuality issues have relation with social criticism in literature. The formulation of social theories into literary studies is able to produce an analysis of gender and sexuality in a number of literary works according to the reality and values that develop in the social life of society. Currently, the Transgender population has gained massive public awareness through social media, films and literature. They have managed to accolade a considerable level of attention globally. This has grown to be a treasured subject matter for dialogue in the modern era. It's a high time to reshape the ideology by cultivating a strong, rational and progressive society towards the genders to have a gender equitable environment. Though it is not the concept of Transgender that is new, but rather the attitudes allowing for its repression. Several studies on Transgender populations from different parts of the world have shown real discrimination and stigma towards Transgender people, which sometimes acts as a barrier to the provision of the required care for them. Lack of access to the required information, legal issues, lack of solutions to fertility problems, financial constraints and psychological and emotional obstacles, together with risk of sexually Transmitted infections all such complications contribute to make their life more difficult. Only some decades ago Transgenderism was considered a psychiatric disease and was classified as "gender identity disorder". That term has been recently replaced by "gender dysphoria" and no longer appears in the Diagnostic and Statistical Manual of Mental Disorders (DMS -5) as a mental illness.

Transgender and Gender Nonconforming Literature

Queer desires have found their way into literature for thousands of years. Authors from Ancient Greece and Rome such as Plato and Homer include love between men in their writing. About India, historian Rana Safvi says:

> "love was celebrated in India in every form whether ancient or medieval India, fluid sexuality was present in the society, one can see the depictions of homosexuality in the temples of Khajurao and Mughal chronicles." [7]

By the late nineteenth and early twentieth centuries, representation of Transgender sexual and romantic desires played a vital role in the development of LGBTQ+ identities. In the world of literature representation of Transgender experiences and identities remain some of the most contested and has many gatekeepers: parents, educators, librarians, even publishers themselves.

Transgender literature generally concerns itself with the triangulated relationship between the body, culture and power (the power to name, to normalise and to efface). Torrey Peter's novel *DeTransition, Baby* (2021) and Maggie Nelson's autobiography *The Argonauts* (2015) in these two Transgender texts, authors represent the body as a heuristic tool; a field against which normative fantasies play out in frequently incongruent ways. Understanding the Transbody as a fertile ground to consider the Transition between stagnation and change between hegemonic and liberatory discourses of gender and sex.

Judith Butler's foundational text, *Gender Trouble: Feminism and the Subversion of Identity* came out to be a scholarly revolution on queer and Transgender studies. Her work represents a radically new take on gender in that it sees beyond binary dualism and challenges its readers to consider not as an ontological status but as an epistemological fabrication. To Butler, gender is not real, but is instead fabricated and culturally reinforced through repetitive gendered acts that interplay with the sexed body. Butler elaborates this idea in the first chapter of *Gender Trouble:*

> "Gender is the repeated stylisation of the body, a set of repeated acts within a highly rigid regulatory frame that congeal over time to produce the appearance of substance, of a natural sort of being. A political genealogy of gender ontologies, if it is successful, will deconstruct the substantive appearance of gender into its constitutive acts and locate and account for those acts within the compulsory frames set by the various forces that police the social appearance of gender." [8]

The quantity and quality of LGBTQ+ literature for young adults reflect shifts in social acceptance which influences their way into dominant culture, and depicts diverse and positive representations to the world. In the twentieth century, *Orlando* (1928) by Virginia Woolf is considered as one of the first Transgender novels in English and whose plot follows a bisexual poet that changes gender from male to female and lives for hundreds of years.

A satirical novel *Myra Breckinridge* published in 1968 by Gore Vidal written in the form of a diary is a controversial book and also "the first instance of a novel in which the main character undergoes a clinical sex change". Critic Harold Bloom cites the novel as a canonical work in his book *The Western Canon*.

An epistolary novel *The Color Purple* by Alice Walker which won the 1983 Pulitzer Prize for Fiction and National Book Award for Fiction is a seminal work in the field of queer literature as well as ground-breaking feminist text questioning religion and identity.

Mahesh Dattani's *On a Muggy Night in Mumbai: a Stage Play* (2013) is the first Indian play boldly dealing with the subject of homosexuality. It deals with the gay themes of love, homosexual vulgarity among the youths in a materialistic world. Zaina Arafat's debut novel *You Exist Too Much* (2020) is the winner of Lambda Literary Award for Bisexual Fiction in 2021. It is an engrossing study of a young, bisexual Palestinian-American woman, who as an adult find herself in a multi-layered struggle of identity, trying to come to terms with her sexuality, gender and culture. Rebecca Makkai's *The Great Believers* (2018), Nicole Dennis – Benn's *Here Comes the Sun* (2016), Alice Oseman's *Heartstopper* (2019), Nina LaCour's *Yerba Buena: A Novel* (2022) etc. are some notable works dealing with such themes.

Trans and Non-binary Children's Literature

Literature has always been a key component in the development of children's linguistic skills and moral awareness. As one of the primary goals of education is to liberate individuals from irrational practices and attitudes, educational content needs to focus on the importance of helping the students to understand the essentials of gender equality. Children's literature plays a critical role in shaping how children view themselves and the world around them. Children's literature that features Transgender and/or nonconforming characters has the capacity to improve attitudes towards the outgroups, but also the self-image of the individuals reading about them.

A few books about boys who challenged gender stereotypes somehow came into popularity by Charlotte Zolotow's *William's Doll* (1979), a story of a little boy who wants a doll. Tomie dePaola's *Oliver Button Is a Sissy* (1979) also tells the story of a boy's desire for a skirt. Lesléa Newman's *Heather Has Two Mommies* (1989) inaugurated a new trend in LGBTQ+ children's literature by representing lesbian families as patterned after heteronormative conventions. Dozens of books about queer families have been published which increased social acceptance and public visibility of lesbian and gay families parallels political discussions about marriage, equality and LGBTQ+ adoption.

Autobiographies and Memoirs

Transgender self-writings are noted for their power of language and revelation. Writers use such genres as a suitable form to express themselves more clearly and deeply. Autobiographies and memoirs provide a platform for the readers to understand and evaluate the writers more intensely and it helps the writers to reveal their trauma to the public and truly picturise their long term suppression and discrimination experienced by them from the gender constructs of society. Literary figures, puns, comparisons, irony, choice of words, sarcasm and monologue indicates an outflow of strong impressions from a swollen and wounded heart. The potential of chosen words are nothing but actual bitter experiences in the life of writer.

The modern Trans memoir came into being with Christine Jorgensen's *A Personal Autobiography* (1967), an American Trans woman who was the first person to become widely known in the United States for having sex reassignment surgery.

Jeanette Winterson's *Oranges Are Not the Only Fruit* (1985) is a semi-autobiographical novel that is a coming-of-age story about a lesbian girl who grows up in an English Pentecostal community. This seminal work questions the concept of sex, gender, religion and faith.

Jamison Green's *Becoming A Visible Man* first published in 2004 remains a beloved resource for Trans people and their allies. In this work Green clarifies Transgender experience for Transgender people and their families and friends with profoundly personal and eminently practical threads. Emphasising the lives of Transgender men who are often overlooked. His inspirational wisdom has informed and empowered thousands of readers. The New York Times called it "The first great memoir by Trans man." [9]

Redefining Realness: My Path to Womanhood, Identity, Love & So Much More (2014) is a memoir and a debut book by an American writer and Transgender activist Janet Mock. This memoir follows author's journey as a Transgender girl and young woman in Hawaii.

I am Vidya: A Transgender's Journey originally published in 2007 is an autobiographical work by Living Smile Vidya. In this work she picturizes the trauma faced by a tirunangai, a Transgender in the society which defines the rights and limits of men and women in terms of biology alone. It was originally written in Tamil and Translated into seven languages. Vidya's narrative clearly suggests the agonies undergone by a woman trapped within a man's body.

Manobi Bandopadhyay, the first PhD professor in India who accepts her identity as a Transgender person, presents herself as a fine specimen offering insights into the mental trauma of Transgender through her book *A Gift of Goddess Lakshmi.* One could see her excellence and mastery in the use of language where she is able to imprint her emotions through a few introspective questions:

> "I am one of them. All my life people have called me *Hijra*, brihannala, napungshak, khoja, Launda ... and I have lived these years knowing that I am an outcast. Did it pain me? It maimed me. But time, to use a cliché, is the biggest healer. The adage worked a little differently in my case. The pain remains but the ache has dulled with time. It visits me in my loneliest hours, when I come face to face with the question of my existential reality. Who am I and why was I born a woman trapped in a man's body? What is my destiny?"[10]

Among many works, The Truth About Me: A Hijra Life Story (2010) by A Revathi, Me Hijra, Me Laxmi (2015) by Laxmi Narayan Tripathi, She's Not There: A Life in Two Genders (2003) by Jennifer Finney Boylan, Bumbling Into Body Hair: A Transsexual's Memoir (2012) by Everett Maroon etc. are some fine pieces to unearth the literary and reformative potentials of Transgender memoirs and autobiographies.

Conclusion

The literary output and reformative capacity of Trans writings are absolutely laudable. Works published in the multiple fields of LGBTQ+ literature, whether it is children's picture books, young adult novels, comics, pulp fiction, autobiographies and memoirs; each genre provide readers a historical overview of the field and introduces readers to key terms, debates and primary concerns of gender issues. Each genre also contextualises the creation, publication, distribution and reception of Trans literature within a shifting sociocultural landscape. The role of literature is immensely influential to visualise gender impartiality through better reasoning and deliberation. It plays a role of crucial determinant and institutional support that can effectively inculcate gender sensitivity that guides a wide range of profits in human society.

References

Boylan, J. F. (2017, June 13) "The Modern Trans Memoir Comes of Age." *The New York Times. https://www.nytimes.com/2017/06/13/books/review/critics-take-queer-writing.html*

Butler, J. (1999) *Gender Trouble: Feminism and Subversion of Identity*. Routledge New York and London. P. 43&44

Harding, S. (1986). *The Science Question in Feminism.* Cornwell Publishing University Press. P. 17

Karlsberg, M. (2018, June 21) "The Importance of Transgender Literature." *San Francisco Bay Times.* https://sfbaytimes.com/importance-Transgender-literature/

Millet, K. (1970) *Sexual Politics*. Doubleday.

Nair, H. R. J. (2021) "Literary Potential and Reformative Power of Transgender Self Writings From India." *Quest Journals: Journal of Research in Humanities and Social Sciences,* Volume 9-Issue 7. *https://www.questjournals.org/jrhss/papers/vol9-issue7/Ser-6/D10071317.pdf*

Pandey, V. (2018, December 31) "Why legalising gay sex in India is not a Western idea." *BBC* https://www.bbc.com/news/world-asia-india-46620242

Schillace, B. (2021, May 10) "The Forgotten History of the World's First Trans Clinic." *Scientific American.* https://www.scientificamerican.com/article/the-forgotten- history-of-the-worlds-first-Trans-clinic/?amp=true

Styker, Susan. & Whittle, Stephen. (2006). *The Transgender Studies Reader.* Routledge Taylor and Francis Group. P. 3.

Wright, A. (2017, December 11) *Neither/Nor: Representations of Transgender Characters in Hindi Films.* https://www.academia.edu/36231413/ Neither_Nor_ Representations _of_Transgen der_Characters_in_Hindi_Films

CHAPTER 6

Transgenders, the Unrecognised Rights and Scuffle

Anya Gonsalves

This paper empirically studies the process of change that has come about throughout the world. The stereotypical mindset about men and women being equal for the most of it is a concern however not as much of one as compared to the outlook people have towards Transgenders. The study of Transgenders has a long history associated with it and as ever day goes by the commendable effort by the world to be more welcoming to these people not belonging to the male and female binary is exemplary. The fine line between identity and gender is now being understood and the rights of these people are being put into place just as they should be. This study conducted through means of research and survey have shown rather how easy it is to have the 3rd gender placed right besides the 1st and 2nd. It has analysed the difficulties faced in the past and has now acknowledged them and the rights that should be given to them as humans along with the obstacles faced on the way.

Introduction

Be it gay, bisexual, lesbian or Transgender people still remain people and that's where the change should start. Gender inequalities has been a long prevailing issue that our society likes to believe has made tremendous provisions for. Transgender community is not only deprived of their basic human right in India but all throughout the world. However, now civil society is raising its voice in support of this community and accordingly we see some changes in the status of this community at international level as well (Bhagat and Saini). Before they are written into legal texts, human rights often emerge from claims of people suffering injustice and thus are based on moral sentiment, culturally determined by contextualised moral and religious belief systems (Marks, 2016). Trans and Transgender are both umbrella terms used to describe people with a wide range of (UN Free & Equal, 2017) gender expressions and identities – including Transsexual people, people who cross-dress, people who identify as third gender, people who identify outside of the male/female binary, and others whose appearance and characteristics are perceived as gender atypical and whose sense of their own gender is different to the sex that they were assigned at birth (UN Free & Equal, 2017). The society is full of intricacies and so are people, but who is that one perfect person who has the right to comment on someone a little different. Growing up traditionally we have been brought up to treat people a certain way but when people change so does our behaviour towards them. Change is not easy and definitely not something one likes to encounter. But without change there is no progress, and for our society to actually develop, progress is a much needed essential for the same. According to studies conducted by various scholars and people it has come to light the discrimination towards the 3rd gender.

Human rights are those rights give to people irrespective of one's nationality, gender, identity, religion, caste or creed then why are people belonging to the Transgender community being denied their basic rights. The right to freedom and expression is one of the most important and basic human rights every individual deserves to have and on no basis can be denied these rights. To name a few human rights that are being infringed are the right to freedom and expression, the right to life and liberty, the right to be treated with humanity, the right to freedom from discrimination, the right to privacy, the right to health, the right to education and the right to work. After 2014 and the Transgender community being recognised as a legal 3rd gender due to the NALSA vs Union of India Case, one would hope that they would now face fewer humiliations and no discrimination but they still have many problems in society. Although the Transgender population is protected by a lot of Regional and international laws and provisions, the poorly framed national laws, practises, policies and provisions towards these people are barely functioning the way they should. Persons with either cisgender (in which assigned and experienced gender are the same) or Transgender identities deserve to live and flourish in their communities – with freedom to learn, work, love, and play – and build lives connected with others at home, in the work place, and in public settings without fear for their safety and survival (Powell et al., 2016).

Methods

To conduct this research and to understand the problems faced by the Transgender people and identify their rights that are being infringed. The method used was that of research and review of literature along with an interview and survey that was conducted which resulted in a list of problems coming to light.

Results

Under the right to equal opportunities at work the Transgender community about 96% of them remains unemployed and this is mainly due to the discrimination they face and the fact that they are denied basic educational rights. Indian society specially is the witness of the sufferings, humiliations, and discriminating treatment against Transgenders from the ancient time. Where one segment of the human fraternity is equipped with all the amenities of life and are planning to visit and make their next home on the moon, *Hijra* community on the other hand are still crying for their recognition as a normal human being. The rapid economic and cultural development of the entire globe could not make a difference in the status of Transgender worldwide and even in the contemporary time they are victimised by social superiors (Bhagat, 2022). Although the number of Transgender persons is small, it should be pointed out that the Transgender community is very diverse. It includes pre-operative and post-operative Transsexual persons, but also persons who do not choose to undergo or do not have access to operations (Commissioner for Human Rights, 2009). According to (Marks, 2016), Ethical and religious precepts determine what one is willing to accept as properly a human right. Such precepts are typically invoked in the debates over current issues such as abortion, same-sex marriage, the death penalty, migration, much as they were around slavery and inequality based on class, gender or ethnicity in the past. Studies have shown that people belonging to the 3rd gender often face discrimination at work and are given fewer opportunities as compared to the rest this is simply because they are being denied another basic human right and that is the right to quality education. The right to education is one basic right that should not be denied to any human irrespective of how they identify themselves. In order to understand the concept of gender identity, it is important to distinguish between the notions of 'sex' and 'gender'. While 'sex' primarily refers to the biological difference between women and men, 'gender' also includes the social aspect of the difference between genders in addition to the biological element (Commissioner for Human Rights, 2009). Although guidelines are pretty expressive about rules and regulations to prevent discrimination towards Transgenders, people still seem to cause problems by denying people to identify as a certain sex and act or use the facilities for the same. While being interviewed they said even though these basic rights being denied comes under the human right laws, they are not paid much attention to and are not of any importance to those in power. They also mentioned how they are mocked when they go for interviews and how some people are still homophobic and refuse to even given them a chance.

The freedom of speech and expression is curbed among the Transgender people simply because the way they present themselves is not acceptable or different from the way others around them behave. In a country like India where its social norms and customs are strongly rooted in its people for how long is the discrimination towards those who are different going to continue because of an ideology that has passed down mostly on the basis of history. Basic health care is denied to most Transgenders because of simple document formalities that eventually decide whether one lives or not. In a state in India a person belonging to the Transgender community simply succumbed to death because hospital authorities could not decide which ward to admit the person to. Often Transgender people choose not to enter the official procedures at all due to discriminatory medical processes and inappropriate treatment, or due to the fact that only one course of treatment is available. They are then, in turn, denied legal recognition of their preferred gender and name, or gender reassignment treatment that fits their own wishes and personal health needs (Commissioner for Human Rights, 2009).

Discussion

After gathering the information, it is pretty evident that even in the 21st century gender inequality is seen. The laws regarding Transgenders and their rights should be specified according to the problems they face and provisions for the same should be made. It is also important to create awareness about the need to educate.

Another uncommon issue is something known as gender dysphoria which is a persistent discomfort with one's biologic sex or assigned gender. In the past few years, GD has received an unprecedented amount of attention in all forms of media, perhaps under the broader rubric of the term's "Transgender" or "Transgenderism." In 2014, an essay in Time suggested that a "tipping point" had been reached with regard to "Transgender visibility (Zucker, Lawrence and Kreukels, 2016). Although people at the time may not be aware of the identity or gender, they would like to be a legal system that makes the Transition smoother will help in this process. To violate someone's human right is to treat that person as though she or he were not a human being. These are basically few natural rights which cannot be denied, but at the same time not guaranteed by Statutory Law (Md. Kamruzzaman and Shashi Kanto Das). Gender identity is one of the most fundamental aspects of life. The sex of a person is usually assigned at birth and becomes a social and legal fact from there on. However, a relatively small number of people experience problems with being a member of the sex recorded at birth (Commissioner for Human Rights, 2009). To defend Transgender rights is to defend the right to choose how one expresses gender and gender identity. Choice, far from being unimportant, is a critical aspect of Transgender rights (Powell et al., 2016). Although the Transgender population is protected by a lot of Regional and international laws and provisions, the poorly framed national laws, practises, policies and provisions towards these people are barely functioning the way they should. The procedure to change one's gender identification documents is a highly taxing task which results in a very limited access to justice as well as basic rights. Commissioner for Human Rights (2009) delineates,

The recognition of gender identity as one of the universally protected discrimination grounds has also been voiced by the UN High Commissioner for Human Rights: "Neither the existence of national laws, nor the prevalence of custom can ever justify the abuse, attacks, torture and indeed killings that gay, lesbian, bisexual, and Transgender persons are subjected to because of who they are or are perceived to be. The claim that human rights are universal holds that they are the same for everyone because they are inherent in human beings by virtue of all people being human, and that human rights therefore derive from nature (hence the term "natural rights"). The UDHR refers to "the inherent dignity and … equal and inalienable rights of all members of the human family [as] the foundation of freedom, justice and peace in the world (Marks, 2016). Along with the Transgender people, those who identify as something they are not born into are almost treated as bad. A common mistake made by everyone is the inability to find the difference between gender, sex and identity. The difference between which is an important thing to understand in order to make a change. The violence towards these people always goes unpunished and why is that so? Isn't there supposed to be justice for all? Why do people find it so hard to include the 3rd gender into the category of all. They are subjected to humiliation, discrimination, assaults, harassment and are victimised in all sectors. According to Marks (2016), Human rights have in common an ethical concern for just treatment, built on empathy or altruism in human behaviour and concepts of justice in philosophy. The philosopher and economist, Amartya Sen, considers that "Human rights can be seen as primarily ethical demands… Like other ethical claims that demand acceptance, there is an implicit presumption in making pronouncements on human rights that the underlying ethical claims will survive open and informed scrutiny.

The historic judgment given by Supreme Court of India in NALSA case entitles him to be equally treated under Indian Constitution. Not only that the verdict gives them right to self-identification i.e., identifying one's gender as male, female, or third gender, and they were to be recognised as socially and economically backward classes, thereby making them eligible for reservations in jobs and educational institutions. The practical implication of this judgment of the Supreme Court is far from the reality and Trans people are bound to live a helpless life in India and facing many problems (Bhagat, 2022). There is a very beautiful concept called the gingerbread person developed by Sam Killermann that beautifully explains the difference between expression, gender, identity and sex and emphasis on what a difference it would make to society if people today were to understand that difference. He created a friendly info graphic that represents the four components of human identity and explains how the terms associated with each category are evolving over time. He talks about the assigned sex of an individual which says that it is the biological classification of a person as male, female or intersex which is usually assigned at birth based on visual assessment and external anatomy. He then explains the second component which is gender identity and the difference between that and sex. He says that it is a person's individual and internal experience of gender which may or may not be visible to others and it may or may not be aligned to what was assigned at birth. The third component he says is gender expression which is a way gender is presented and communicated to the world through clothing, speech, body language, hairstyle, voice and/or the emphasis or (Egale, 2020) de-emphasis of body characteristics and behaviours. The fourth component is attraction and is simply referred to as referred to as a sexual orientation, attraction describes a person's potential for emotional, spiritual, intellectual, intimate, romantic and/or sexual interest in other people and may form the basis for aspects of one's identity and/or behaviour (Egale, 2020).

Now the need to understand this classification is to be more gender sensitive and realise that a society no longer consists of only men and women. He states that understanding this classification will help society make better laws and provisions for people belonging to it in order to make the society more inclusive. Being inclusive in society only means accepting the LGBTQ+ community more openly and with more understanding. Another major issue under family law is that of the way it is laid down, India is a country where in live in relationships are not wrong but neither right too. In this case there are no laws to protect those except that of the protection of women from domestic violence only if they have been in that live in relationship for over a period of years. This law firmly lays down the fact that it will be applicable only in the case of a man and women staying together and is therefore discriminatory to the people belonging to the Transgender or LGBTQ+ community. Why do we have certain laws that are not applicable to all the members of its society when the goal is to be progressive and develop the country is a question that leaves people pondering?

The right to privacy has been fully encroached in terms of the Transgender community. By protecting a person from uninvited intrusion, privacy ensures that a person can live with dignity. Transgender persons are usually thrown out from their homes as family refuses to accept them and are forced to live on the streets as accommodation for these people has been made difficult. They are either given a certain way in which they are supposed to live while renting out a premises or are usually used for sex work. A very recent news articles shows three Transgender persons who used to begin Udupi and Manipal city areas have now started a canteen at the city bus stand that functions from 1am to 7am in order to quench the hunger and thirst of night travellers and those who work in night shift. They have received a good amount of customers who treat them with respect and have proved to the rest of the world that it is possible to get away from these evils and even when family and society does not accept them, they are able to create a live worth living for themselves and live with dignity and peace. When it comes to employment the people who don't identify as female or males in the gender binary are usually the ones facing maximum discrimination when it comes to gender discrimination and employment. As they continue to fight for an equal place in society, that includes equal opportunities at workplaces. As we know employees get certain benefits such as medical insurances, security clearances etc. But when people start identifying or changing their gender to the 3rd sex they often tend to be denied with these basic requirements and no provisions are made for them to have a happy and comfortable work environment. Gender nonconformity is another concept that could have implications on people's well-being. This could be very stressful for many gender minority individuals, and perhaps more so for those with experiences of harassment and violence (UCLA 2013). The concept gender nonconformity generally refers to the perception that one's expression of gender is different from societal norms through comparisons with and pressure received by peers, family, and other important members of their social networks. These studies have linked gender nonconformity to experiences of victimisation and distress within nonTrans gender populations. (UCLA 2013)

Conclusion

What is a pivotal path to development? The simple way to address the question would be to have social inclusion, acceptance and equality in society. Many countries around the world are now becoming sensitive on Transgender issue and enacting laws protecting their rights. It is now high time to break the general myth that the human society can be based only on binary structure of male and female and will have to accommodate Transgenders in our social framework (Bhagat, 2022). States are obliged to respect, protect and fulfil the human rights of all persons within their jurisdiction, including LGBTI persons. These obligations extend to refraining from interference in the enjoyment of rights; preventing abuses by

State agencies and officials, private corporations and individuals; monitoring, investigating and combating such abuses when they occur; and providing remedy to victims (UN Free & Equal, 2017).

The psychological and sociological factors that are involved must be taken highly into consideration as it is truly unfair to those facing these kinds of problems. Gender based discrimination has become a very persistent culture in most parts over the world and while they slowly try to improve these conditions it must be taken more seriously to actually bring about change. The invisibility of gender minority people plays a large role in the health disparities they experience. The authors of this study found that the gender Transition/gender identity questions could be a useful tool in identifying gender minority populations while minimising misunderstandings among gender majority populations Badgett, et al. (2014).

The government can help people by funding small organisations of women and Transgenders. Empower them and support their leadership. Make education gender sensitive. Give proper value to work by women and Transgenders. Encourage them to get into non-traditional vocations. The main focus should be on performance and if they are able and willing to work hard to produce outcomes that will be profitable, they should not be discriminated based on biological sex. Understand and educate others about the difference in gender and biological sex and help them respect people based on the same. Women and Transgenders lack the voice and ability to partake in decisions that affect them and their families and their economic opportunities tend to remain constrained. Thus, addressing gender inequalities it's not only the right thing to do but also the smart thing to do (Canada : Budget 2018). Studies show that gender progress doesn't benefit an individual but the society as a whole. One will be able to see a society actually prosper when men, women and Transgenders are equally empowered. This should be promoted at a young age when people say a particular activity is only for the boys, it is important to educate boys and girls about the same so that they can practise and preach what was taught to them when they were young. When women and Transgenders are treated equally, they will automatically feel the need to perform better and have a healthier work environment, motivating them to produce good outcomes and work to the best of their abilities. Some great examples of people belonging to this community by an article by India today are Sathyasri

Sharmila who became the country's first Transgender attorney. She set an example by choosing to pursue law so that she could combat injustice, rejecting the stereotypical mindset in the process. Prithika Yashini defied all odds to become the first Transgender sub-inspector despite being ruled unsuccessful by one mark. She had her physical examination score reevaluated, nevertheless, and this time she passed with flying colours. On June 7, 2015, the lovely Manabi Bandopadhyay of Krishnagar Women's College became the first Transgender college principal. She currently holds the position of professor and made history by becoming the first Transgender person to (Olito & Shaw, 2022) earn a doctorate in India (PhD). She has formerly worked as a Bengali associate professor at Vivekananda Satobarshiki Mahavidyalaya.

References

Badgett, M. L., Baker, K. E., Conron, K. J., Gates, G. J., Gill, A., Greytak, E., & Herman, J. L. (2014). "Best practices for asking questions to identify Transgender and other gender minority respondents on population-based surveys (GenIUSS)." *The GenIUSS Group, UCLA Williams Institute.*

Bhagat, P. K. (2022). *A Comparative Study of Rights of Transgender under Human Rights Regime.* ResearchGate | Find and share research. Retrieved April 23, 2023, fromhttps://www.researchgate.net/publication/358426297_A_Comparative_Study_of_Rights_of_Transgender_under_Human_Rights_Regime

Canada: Budget 2018: *Equality and Growth for the Middle Class in Waterloo.* (2018, March 1). MENA Report.

Centre for Women and Democracy. (2014). *Sex & Power 2014: Who Runs Britain?* Barrow Cadbury Trust. Retrieved April 23, 2023, from https://barrowcadbury.org.uk/wp-content/uploads/2014/09/Sex-and-Power-2014.pdf

Commissioner for Human Rights. (2009). *Human rights and gender identity,.* Coucil of Europe. Retrieved April 23, 2023, from https://rm.coe.int/human-rights-and-gender-identity-issue-paper-commissioned-and-publishe/16806da753

Durbin, S. (2010). "Gender inequality in employment: Editors' introduction." *Equality, Diversity and Inclusion: An International Journal, 29*(3), 221-238. https://doi.org/10.1108/02610151011028831

Egale. (2020, February 2). *The Genderbread Person.* Retrieved April 23, 2023, from https://egale.ca/wp-content/uploads/2020/02/ENG-Genderbread-Person_NEW.pdf

Fleetwood, S. (2008a), "Structure, institution, agency, habit and reflexive deliberation", Journal *of Institutional Economics*, Vol. 4 No. 2, pp. 183- 203.

Fleetwood, S. (2008). Institutions and social Structures. *Journal for the Theory of Social Behaviour, 38*(3), 241-265. https://doi.org/10.1111/j.1468-5914.2008.00370.x

Forret, M. L., & Dougherty, T. W. (2004). "Networking behaviors and career outcomes: differences for men and women?." *Journal of Organisational Behavior: The International Journal of Industrial, Occupational and Organisational Psychology and Behavior*, 25(3), 419-437.

Ho, F., & Mussap, A. J. (2019). "The gender identity scale: Adapting the gender unicorn to measure gender identity." *Psychology of Sexual Orientation and Gender Diversity*, *6*(2), 217-231. https://doi.org/10.1037/sgd0000322

India Today. (2018, July 3). *8 Indian Transgender people who were the firsts in their fields.* Retrieved April 23, 2023, from https://www.indiatoday.in/education-today/gk-current-affairs/story/list-of-Transgenders-firsts-who-made-it-big-in-their-fields-1276415-2018-07-03

International Commission of Jurists. (2019). *Sexual Orientation, Gender Identity and International Human Rights Law.* Refworld | The Leader in Refugee Decision Support. Retrieved April 23, 2023, from https://www.refworld.org/pdfid/4a783aed2.pdf

Kamruzzaman, M., & Das, S. K. (2016). "The evaluation of human rights: An overview in historical perspective." *American Journal of Service Science and Management*, *3*(2), 5-12.

Lombardi, E. (2013). *Examination of Gender Identity and Expression Final Report for Williams Institute.* ResearchGate | Find and share research. Retrieved April 23, 2023, from https://www.researchgate.net/publication/258112182_ Examination_of_Gender_Identity_and_Expression_Final_Report_for_Williams_In stitute

Marks, S. P. (2016). *Human rights: A brief introduction.*

Olito, F., & Shaw, G. (2022, June 24). *19 Transgender and non-binary celebrities who are changing television.* Insider. https://www.insider.com/Trans-celebrities-in-television-2019-10

Powell, T., Shapiro, S., & Stein, E. (2016). *Transgender rights as human rights.* Journal of Ethics | American Medical Association. Retrieved April 23, 2023, from https://journalofethics.ama-assn.org/article/Transgender-rights-human-rights/2016-11

Roy, M. (2027). "Gender sensitisation a pillar to sustainable development." WELCOME TO IJCR | *International Journal of Current Research.* Retrieved April 23, 2023, from https://www.journalcra.com/article/gender-sensitisation-pillar-sustainable-development

UN Free & Equal. (2017, October 11). *Definitions.* Retrieved April 23, 2023, from https://www.unfe.org/definitions/

Zucker, K. J., Lawrence, A. A., & Kreukels, B. P. (2016). "Gender dysphoria in adults." *Annual Review of Clinical Psychology*, 12, 217-247.

CHAPTER 7

Confrontational Aspects of Transgender Education in India

Manisha Bose and Soumik Bose

By the spirit of the Constitution of India, all citizens should have an Same chance to grow and reach their potential, regardless of gender, caste, or religion. Anyone can identify their gender. Male, female, and Transgender are the three genders in India. The Transgender community is a component of society and is entitled to the same opportunities as everyone else. Such Transgender people are not a recent phenomenon; their existence has been documented throughout history. Transgender people once enjoyed respect from the general public, but this has changed, and they are now subject to harassment and discrimination. Now that the Right to Education Act of 2009 has been implemented, Transgender people will to be able to go to school and universities with every amenity authorising their admittance as a "disadvantaged group" (RTE). Those who are economically deprived and students are classified as EWS. Category Transsexual individuals are qualified for a 20% admissions reservation. Even though they aren't notably recognised, many Transgender people carried the torch for historical changes. Their prejudice has always been a problem and has grown flimsier. They will receive educational and employment opportunities, the Supreme Court declared, as OBCs reservations. Transgender people are excluded from social and cultural activities and are despised by society and family. The current the Transgender community's economic, social, and job position in India has been examined in this paper.

Introduction

The term "Transgender" describes people who do not fit neatly into one of the binary gender categories. Such opposition is made possible by the shattered and muddled traditional gender norms pervasive in the culture. Castrated guys who belong to the third gender have a lengthy history dating ahead to the ninth century BC. They were generally used as guards in the imperial quarters for ladies, these newly castrated men. Another issue under Article 21 is the freedom to select gender identification, which is a necessary component of living a life of dignity. The Court noted that "the gender to which a person belongs is to be determined by the person concerned" while determining the privilege of privacy freedom and self-determination. A court has granted gender identity rights to the people of India. 'Transgender' refers to a broad spectrum of identities, outward manifestations, and conduct that blur or crosses gender boundaries. Cross-dressers (previously known as Transvestites), who dress in clothing usually connected with the "opposite" gender; cross-dressing drag kings and queens in Gender queers, who identify as something other than a binary gender or sex system, and performers are all included under this Transgender umbrella. Where Transgender students have participated in campus life particular concerns, this article explores What Transgender students go through, and how student affairs professionals can help successfully meet these students' needs. programming, accommodation, restrooms, changing rooms, counselling, medical care, records, and paperwork. Student affairs professionals must be aware of the challenges that Transgender students face at most colleges and universities since, as this field has shown, they frequently experience institutional prejudice in higher education.

Transgender Education Status

Transgender is a third gender recognised by the Indian Constitution. This new sex is becoming more and more popular. Since they are excluded from social and cultural activities, they have limited access to facilities like schools, hospitals, and public spaces, denying them the constitutional rights to Equal protection under the law and before the law.

Statutory Status

The intention is to accommodate the Transgender student. However, no formal schooling for Transgender people is standard in India in such circumstances.

A school would frequently give a single room for the student on a floor with mixed genders and, if. Access to a private bathroom may be possible

Transgenderity in Education

Concerns regarding How their pupils will behave respond and whether they are Transgender may influence recruiting and decisions about tenure must be considered by faculty Transitioning while working. But significantly, Transgender studies are becoming increasingly valued as academic research.

Bathrooms

Transgender students and staff in secondary education experience many of the same challenges as Trans people have in higher education, such as security issues, access to bathrooms and healthcare, and the correct identification of gender on documents. The usage of public restrooms is another instance of discrimination against Transgender individuals Lesbians, however, and other females who appear masculine, are frequently harassed in female bathrooms, which is also a problem for Transsexual women, who are particularly affected by the "bathroom issue."

Both Women identifying as Transgender and other gender variants are entitled to restroom use. that corresponds to they are male, and non-Transgender women ought to feel secure during this private-public spaces.

College officials who have handled restroom disputes have attempted to strike a balance between the needs of Transgender individuals' person and the complaint while also acknowledging that a Trans person Access should never be denied decent washroom facilities due to the bias of a third party.

Assignment of Gender to College Records

On school records, Transgender people can encounter discrimination in the educational system.

Transgender advocates are starting to pressure school administrators to use more inclusive language as they recognise. They asked students, staff, and faculty to indicate whether they were male or female on college registration. However, personnel forms ignore the subtleties of gender and imply that those who identify as gender nonconforming do not belong at the institution.

Illiteracy-Related Problems with a Zero Acceptance Level

In practically every aspect of their lives, members of the Transgender community experience severe stigma and discrimination. Particularly during their formative years, Transgender people experience physical, sexual, and emotional neglect and discrimination-related violence. They frequently suffer from abuse and isolation and are forbidden from using the same playground as their peers. When effeminate males are accused of breaking social and academic norms by teachers, families and schools, they turn into torture rooms for them.

Forced Illegality

Transgender people who are excluded from family and school drop out reduce their options for employment. This deprivation is the primary factor contributing to the increased drop-out rates among the Transgender community, according to reports and interviews with community members and stakeholders. A Transgender person often holds a second or senior secondary (Matriculation) degree. The enrollment is noticeably Low and the rates of primary and secondary school dropouts remain relatively high. For the community, closing the gap between socioeconomic exclusion and gender inequality is still a significant concern.

Impatience and Need for Counsel

Teachers condemn Transgender people, guided by widespread societal norms and stigmas. Teachers' insensitivity negatively impacts the Transgender community. Transgender people lose access to their families and the educational setting, stop their education and put their future employment prospects in danger. A comprehensive examination of numerous reports and discussions with the community and stakeholders lead to the conclusion that Transgender people tend to be undereducated or illiterate, which makes them reluctant to continue their education. Most teaching fraternity members are ignorant of and insensitive to Transgender concerns. Secondary (Matric) or upper secondary level qualifications are the norm. The enrollment is noticeably low, and the primary and secondary dropout rates are still very high. They need to acquire more education since they are neither socially accepted nor well-educated Even if they are enrolled in a school, they regularly experience harassment and bullying and are either asked to leave or decide to drop out on their own. This is why they start begging and doing sex jobs. The government is required to give Transgender pupils inclusive education and adult education.

Community Status

Because of stigma and discrimination, the Transgender community has fewer possibilities than others. They do not acquire a proper education because they need to be socially accepted and well-educated. Even if they are enrolled in a school, they regularly experience harassment and bullying and are either asked to leave or decide to drop out on their own. This is why they start begging and doing sex jobs. They commit to unprotected sexual activity out of fear of rejection or a desire to farm their gender via sex, which forces them into sex work that puts them at the highest risk of catching HIV.

Controversies with Social Acceptance

Denial and hostility toward Transgender persons can start right at home. The issues vary from seclusion, rejection, and denial of family property to verbal and physical violence. Transgender people are frequently stigmatised and rejected by society due to their sexual orientation or gender identification. Social stigma includes being disempowered due to the labelling and unfavorable/generalised perception of those individuals who are compelled to perform as sex workers or sex solicitors.

Living Rooms

Transgender students may experience housing and roommate challenges, as well as toilet issues, when living in residence halls, particularly single-sex ones. Numerous universities deal with gender issues and are reluctant to cooperate to ensure education. A Transgender person does not receive enough support from instructors and other adults because their family and society already reject them. Consequently, they were compelled to stop their schooling immediately.

Transgender Education's Problems

The term "third gender" is problematic in and of itself since it views sexuality as a ladder, with the queer community occupying the bottom rung. Although it gives them legal recognition, it does not improve their situation because they continue to belong to a socially excluded group and are not treated equally to the rest of the Indian people. While it is crucial to highlight the many ways that the inclusion principle has failed, India has now been able to put the long-hoped-for but ineffective idea into practice.

The Use of Derogatory Names and Pronouns

Being disrespectful on purpose means continuing to use a last name and other pronouns. As long as it is consistent, good faith progress in using the correct name and pronouns, Transgender youth can comprehend and empathise with some uncertainty.

School, College and University Includsion

It might be challenging to include Transgender students in both high school and college. Giving Transgender pupils the same educational opportunities as other students of the same gender is extremely difficult due to the inclusion issue with male and female students.

Imperfect Personality

Young people who identify as Trans feel lonely a lot. Few libraries provide information on biological sex and gender, gender identity, or being Transgender, and few youth-oriented programmers hire Transgender persons.

Privacy

If their gender identity or gender expression is revealed to the family, Transgender youth may have hostile families and potentially experience violence and expulsion from their homes.

Access to Appropriate Restroom Facilities is Limited

There is a need for a concentrated institutionalised mechanism of research and academic activities to produce more data/information to identify and understand the problems related to different facets of their lives and to assist in formulating policies through research and academic programs that would bring about an effective and long-term change in their lives.

Conclusion

People who identify as Transgender often experience discrimination and harassment at home, school, and in the community, which compels them to relocate. The type of harassment encompasses verbal, physical, and sexual assault, all of which significantly negatively influence one's mental health. Transgender people cannot exercise their social and political rights in a democratic nation like India. They do not participate in any welfare programs. Discrimination and equitable access to amenities and healthcare must be addressed if institutions are hospitable to persons of all genders

References

Bolich, G. G. (2010). *Transgender History and Geography Crossdressing in Context,* Vol.3. North Carolina: Psyche's Press.

Law, T. (2005). Policy Institute. "Ways that Colleges and Universities Meet the Needs of Transgender students.". *Transgender Law and Policy Institute.* "College and University Policies." www.Transgenderlaw.org/college.

Rajesh, D., & Naved, A. (2013). *Approach paper on education and employment opportunities and challenges for Transgender.* New Delhi, India: National Expert Committee on Issues of Trans gender Persons, Ministry of Social Justice and Empowerment, Government of India.

Sadashiv. P (2012). *Rights of Transgender People: Sensitising of cars to Provide Access to Justice.* Http://www.hcmadrs.tn.nic.in/academy/Article/PSJ-CJO-SPEECH-Royappetah.pdf Wikipedia, The free encyclopedia retrieved from http://en.m.wikipedia.org/wiki/Transgender.

Stryker, S. (2008). *Transgender History.* Seal Press: United States of America

CHAPTER 8

Recognition of Transgenders: A Critical Analysis of the Rights of Transgender in G20 Countries

Nikita Nimbalkar

Gender equality has been emphasised in almost all corners of the globe. However, when it comes to gender quality or identification, only binary consideration has been given, neglecting the third gender, i.e. Transgender or LGBTQ community. Prejudices and social stigma are widespread in many cultures, and social attitudes towards Transgender people and other members of the gender minority vary worldwide. The community has been in the minority and neglected throughout history. The study attempts to understand the legal identification of the Transgender community in the 19 countries of the G20 Members. It is observed that most countries recognise the Transgender community but lack protection laws. Some of the G20 countries have official figures on the population of Transgenders, but none of the countries has exact data as the population is also considered a hidden population. The hidden population exists because of a lack of protection by the government, appropriate implementation of the laws and discrimination in society. Many countries, including India, do not have legal provisions on same-sex marriage, and the true sense of inclusivity or gender diversity is missing. Although there have been improvements in Transgender laws and protection over time, there is still a long way to go for all of us.

Introduction

A person who identifies as Transgender is one whose (Peterson, n.d.) gender identity differs from their sex at birth. From the moment of their birth, their gender conduct or identity does not correspond with their biological sex. They experience more discrimination and violence than people of other genders since they have been the most forgotten, neglected, and disadvantaged groups not only in just Indian society but at the global level as well. As discrimination and violence against Transgender are evident, the community faces the basic right of recognition in many countries. The Transgender or non-binary community is frequently facing issues with fundamental rights like the right to life, and to live in freedom and safety (Amnesty International UK, 2017), the right to live free from torture and degrading treatment, the right to health, the right to inclusive education, the right to an adequate standard of living.

For the period of December 1 2022 to November 30 2023, India is the G20's president. The Group of Twenty (G20) is the premier forum for economic cooperation on a global scale. It plays a significant role in forming and strengthening global architecture and governance on all significant international economic issues.

According to the MENA Report (2023), The Group of Twenty (G20) has 19 member countries (Argentina, Australia, Brazil, Canada, China, France, Germany, India, Indonesia, Italy, Japan, Republic of Korea, Mexico, Russia, Saudi Arabia, South Africa, Turkey, United Kingdom, and United States) and the European Union. The G20 members represent around 85% of the global GDP, over 75% of the global trade, and about two-thirds of the world population (MENA Report, 2023).

G20 focuses on socio-economic issues such as agriculture, anti-corruption, climate, digital economy, education, employment, energy, environment, health, tourism, trade and investment. The Working Groups under this track include a Culture Working Group, a Development Working Group, an Employment Working Group, a Health Working Group, etc. W20 (Women 20) is a G20 official engagement organisation that was created in 2015 while Turkey held the G20 chair. Its principal goal is to make sure that gender issues are considered in G20 discussions and reflected in the Leaders' Declaration of the G20 as commitments to policies and practices that advance gender equality and women's economic empowerment. But for gender equality, it only had W20; it is absolutely missing the gender-diverse approach. G20 has clearly defined priorities wiz; Green Development, Climate Finance & Lifestyle for Environment (LiFE), Accelerated, Inclusive & Resilient Growth, Accelerating progress on Sustainable Development Goals (SDGs), Technological Transformation & Digital Public Infrastructure, Multilateral

Institutions for the 21st century (MENA Report, 2023). Women-led development. Gender diversity or inclusivity approach for the third gender is missing the priorities of G20. Thus, this research studies the legal recognition of Transgenders in the G20 countries.

The term "Gender-diverse" is used to describe people whose gender identity, including how they express it, conflicts with what is seen as the gender norm in each situation at a given time, including people who do not identify as either male or female; the more specific term "Trans" is used to describe people who identify with a different sex than the one assigned to them at birth (United Nations, 2023).

According to the ILGA's 2020 Report on State-Sponsored Homophobia6, 124 UN members had completely decriminalised homosexual activities, while 67 U.N. members still criminalised same-sex relationships. Furthermore, capital punishment for these crimes is still prescribed in Yemen, Iran, Saudi Arabia, Mauritania, Nigeria, and Brunei. The report also states that freedom of expression in matters relating to Transgender people is prohibited in 42 U.N. member countries. The constitutions of U.N. members and one non-UN member include safeguards against discrimination based on sexual orientation. Same-sex marriages are legal in 28 U.N. member countries, a non-UN member country, and 30 non-independent territories. Hence, there is no research paper which clearly emphasises on the legal/ constitutional rights of Transgender in G20 countries.

Methodology

The study is based on secondary research, and the research is purely qualitative. Analytical and doctrinal research methods were used in this paper. It provided a critical analysis of G20 countries' process for recognising the rights of the Transgender community. To understand the trend, the official reports of the mentioned countries, news articles and reports of multilateral institutions like the world bank have been referred.

Result and Analysis

India

According to the 2011 Indian Census, approximately 4.88 lakh Transgender people are living in India.

Article 14 of the Indian Constitution essentially grants a fundamental right to equality; while Articles 15 and 16 states that no one shall be subjected to sex discrimination. As part of significant rulings that recognise Transgender people as a third gender, the Indian judiciary also decriminalised Section 377 of the Indian Penal Code. To protect Transgender person's rights, India also passed the Transgender Protection Act 2019. The Act forbids discrimination against Transgender people in areas like employment and education. The right to self-identify as a Trans person is also included. People can apply online for a "Transgender I.D." to the National Portal for Transgender Persons (NPTP), which was created. But the issue of forced sex-reassignment surgeries, which were administered to Transgender people against their will, was not addressed by this Act. The Transgender community does not have an equal marriage act at present in India as it does not recognise registered marriage or civil unions for same-sex couples (Bareque, 2023). However, same-sex couples can attain rights and benefits as a live-in couple (analogous to cohabitation) as per a Supreme Court of India judgement in August 2022 (Bareque, 2023).

Argentina

There are no official figures on the size of Argentina's Transgender community because it was not included in the 2010 census. However, LGBTQ organisations estimate that Argentina's population of 44 million includes 12,000 to 13,000 Transgender adults.

On the one hand, Transgender rights in Argentina have been lauded by many as some of the world's most progressive. The Asociación de Lucha por la Identidad Travesti-Transsexual was founded in 1997 to advocate for the rights and equality of Transgender people in Argentina. Argentina passed its Gender Identity Law, known in Spanish as La Ley de Identidad de Género, in 2012, ensuring that everyone in Argentina has the right to be recognised for their chosen gender identity. Transgender people in Argentina can now identify with their preferred gender on official documents without having to undergo hormone therapy or gender reassignment surgery or face other obstacles such as psychiatric counselling. The law also mandated that all medical facilities, both public and private, provide gender reassignment surgery and hormone therapy to anyone who requests it. Furthermore, the World

Health Organisation praised Argentina in November 2016 for taking significant, exceptional steps towards ensuring Transgender equality.

Australia

The 2016 Census was a significant step forward in collecting Australian statistics on sex and gender diversity. In Australia, the 2016 Census counted 1,260 people who were sex and/or gender diverse. Due to limitations in the special procedures and the willingness or opportunity to report as sex and/or gender diverse, this count is not considered accurate.

Transgender people in Australia are legally protected from discrimination under the Sex Discrimination Act. This Act, which went into effect in 2013, made discrimination based on a person's "gender identity" illegal. This term is defined in Section 5B of the Sex Discrimination Act: "gender identity" means a person's gender-related identity, appearance or mannerisms, or other gender-related characteristics, with or without regard to the person's designated sex at birth. The Sex Discrimination Act of 1984 was amended in 2013 to include new protections against discrimination based on sexual orientation, gender identity, and intersex (M4BL, 2021) status in many areas of public life. These legal safeguards are supplemented by the Australian Government Guidelines on Sex and Gender Recognition, which went into effect in July 2013. The guidelines acknowledge that individuals may identify as a gender other than the one assigned to them at birth or (Queen's University, 2023) may not identify as exclusively male or female. This should be reflected in government records. The guidelines also standardise the evidence required to change a person's sex/gender in personal records held by Australian Government departments and agencies.

Brazil

There is currently no Gender Identity Bill in the Brazilian Congress. Following the reasoning of the IACHR, Brazil's Supreme Court issued a landmark decision in Direct Unconstitutionality Lawsuit 4275 on March 1, 2018, allowing Transgender individuals to change their legal name and gender marker in official documents through an administrative solution. The Court ruled that no psychological evaluation, hormonal treatment, Transition surgery, or other medical procedure is required for this change.

Brazil has seen some growth compared to a decade ago but still lacks Transgender protection regarding legislation against violence and mental health issues within their Transgender community.

According to the TGEU (Transgender Europe) report, 70% of all Transgender murders occurred in Central and South America, with Brazil accounting for 33%. Even though Transphobia is now a crime in Brazil, the country still has the highest number of Trans and queer people murdered worldwide. Brazil topped the list for the 13th year in a row in 2021. Pinheiro (2022) says, the total number of Trans women and queer people murdered has reached an all-time high since data collection began in 2008.

Canada

According to 2021 senses, of the nearly 30.5 million people living in private households in Canada aged 15 and older in May 2021, 100,815 were Transgender (59,460) or non-binary (41,355), accounting for 0.33% of the population in this age group. Generation Z (born between 1997 and 2006, 0.79%) and millennials (born between 1981 and 1996, 0.51%) had three to seven times the proportion of Transgender and non-binary people as Generation X (born between 1966 and 1980, 0.19%), baby boomers (born between 1946 and 1965, 0.15%), and the Interwar and Greatest Generations (born in 1945 or earlier, 0.12%). The Government of Canada (2022) reports, Article 1 of the Universal Declaration of Human Rights declares that "all human beings are born free and equal in dignity and rights." Article 2 declares, "Everyone is entitled to all the rights and freedoms outlined in this Declaration" (Government of Canada, 2022). "All people, including LGBTQ2I individuals, are entitled to the protection provided by international human rights law, which is based on equality and non-discrimination" (Government of Canada, 2022). Prior to 1969, same-sex sexual activities between consenting adults in Canada were considered crimes punishable by imprisonment. According to Heritage (2022) the year, the Canadian government passed an omnibus bill decriminalising private sexual acts between two people over the age of 21 – a watershed moment in the legal treatment of gay men, lesbians, and bisexuals. The Civil Marriage Act passed in 2005, marked a watershed moment in sexual orientation equality rights by allowing same-sex couples to marry anywhere in Canada.

China

There are no official statistics in China on the size of the Transgender population. In China, there are approximately 400 000 Transgender people. Local courts in China are frequently hostile to Transgender people's aspirations.

The National Health Commission's most resented policy on sex reassignment surgery, published in 2017, sets a high bar for access to surgery. Treatment is only available to people over the age of 20, who must first obtain parental permission and undergo psychological and psychiatric therapies for at least a year. Due to these policies, Transgender people face significant challenges in China. They are vulnerable and marginalised because they lack legal recognition and protection. Social stigma and discrimination are prevalent in many schools, universities, businesses, and government offices. The Human Rights Watch (2021) Report says, the research team discovered that while Chinese Transgender people can change their names and gender markers on official identity documents, they must first undergo gender-affirming surgeries.

France

According to the research (Maud Garnier, Sarah Ollivier, Marie Flori, and Christine Maynié-François, 2012) in France, between 1300 and 6500 people self-identify as Transgender (between 0.002% and 0.01% of the general population), that is, with a gender identity or gender expression other than the sex assigned at birth. However, there is no official data available.

Transgender rights in France have been among some of the most progressive in the world. Gender identity disorder was removed as a diagnosis in France by decree in 2010, nothing changed, according to French Transgender rights organisations, aside from the impact of the announcement itself. Discrimination based on sexual identity has been prohibited since 2012. The term sexual identity was replaced by gender identity in 2016 (Wikipedia, 2023). The French Senate approved a bill on November 6, 2015, allowing Transgender people to legally change their gender without the need for sex reassignment surgery (Wikipedia, 2023) or forced sterilisation. The National Assembly approved the bill in May 2016. Transphobia was designated an aggravating factor for all crimes punishable by imprisonment in 2017.

Germany

Transgender people could align their first names with their gender identity after the passage of the 'Transsexuellen-Gesetz' (Transsexuals Act) in 1980. However, lengthy expert hearings were required for this, and Transgender individuals were not allowed to marry or, if already married, had to file for divorce; they were also required to be incapable of procreation or be sterilised and undergo operations to adjust their body image.

Previously, German law mandated that parents give their child a gender-specific name. This is no longer the case, as the Federal Constitutional Court of Germany ruled in 2008 that there is no requirement for a name to be gender-specific. In November 2017, the German Federal Constitutional Court (FashionUnited, 2019) ruled that civil status law must allow for a third gender option, which means that intersex people would have an option other than being listed as female or male or having a blank gender entry. The government presented a proposal on the subject in August 2018. People who are intersex would be able to register as "divers" on official documents. The Bundestag approved the resulting third-gender law in December 2018, and it became effective on January 1, 2019.

Green Party members Nyke Slawik and Tessa Ganserer were elected to the Bundestag in September 2021. They identify as Transgender women. Later that year, the government promised to relax restrictions on legal name changes and compensate Transgender people who had been sterilised against their will.

Indonesia

Transgender people in Indonesia face legal challenges. Traditional values oppose homosexuality and Transitioning, which impacts public policy. Although homosexuality is frowned upon in Indonesia, it is not illegal, except for the ultra-conservative, autonomous province of Aceh. Same-sex couples and households headed by same-sex couples ("LGBT Rights in Bulgaria," 2023) in Indonesia are not entitled to any legal protections afforded to opposite-sex married couples. Indonesia's parliament passed a new criminal code in December 2022 (Human Rights Watch, 2023), making all sex outside of marriage punishable by up to a year in prison. Parents or children can report unmarried couples to the police if they suspect them of having sex under the new law. According to activists, the law would expose same-sex couples to prosecution because they lack the legal right to marry. The law will not be implemented until 2025.

Italy

There is no official data available on the Transgender population in Italy.

Since 1982, Transgender people have been legally allowed to change their gender. Although sexual orientation discrimination in employment has been prohibited since 2003, no other anti-discrimination laws about sexual orientation or gender identity and expression have been enacted nationally, even though some Italian regions have enacted far more comprehensive anti-discrimination laws.

Since 1890, when a new Penal Code was enacted, both male and female same-sex sexual activity has been legal in Italy. In May 2016, a civil union law was passed, granting same-sex couples many of their marriage rights. On the other hand, Stepchild adoption was left out of the bill and is currently being litigated. The same law grants several legal rights to both same-sex and heterosexual couples who live in unregistered cohabitation.

Japan

The poll was conducted on 428,000 people aged 20 to 69 by the Japan LGBT Research Institute Inc., a Tokyo-based think tank specialising in issues concerning sexual minorities. It received 348,000 valid responses, with approximately 10% identifying as LGBT or another sexual minority. Regarding sexual orientation, 2.8 per cent identified as bisexual, while 1.4 per cent admitted to having doubts about their sexuality. In both cases, the proportion of people who identified as asexual or gay was 0.9 per cent.

In Japan, altering an individual's legal gender is archaic and detrimental. Japan bases its laws on the obsolete and derogatory concept that a Transgender identity is a mental health issue. It compels Transgender people seeking formal recognition to undergo lengthy, costly, intrusive, and irreversible medical treatments.

Japan's Gender Identity Disorder Special Cases Act of 2003 violates international human rights law and medical best practices. The Japanese government enacted legislation in 2004 allowing

Transgender people to change their gender officially in their family registers, and the number of people doing so has steadily increased.

Mexico

Last year, Mexico's national statistics agency (INEGI) conducted its first comprehensive Census on sexual and gender diversity. Mexico has published the findings of its first national survey on sexual diversity. Over 5 million people identified as members of the LGBTQ community. That equates to one in every twenty Mexicans over the age of 15.

Under the Napoleonic Code, same-sex marriage has been legal in Mexico since 1871. In 2003, federal legislation to prevent and eliminate discrimination included "sexual preferences" as a protected class. Mexican legislation now makes it the second Latin American country to outlaw discrimination against LGBT people. The Mexican constitution went into effect in 2011. In 2015, the first identical-sex marriage was legalised, and it was declared that any other states that disagreed would be guilty of discrimination and face legal consequences. The Mexican Court issued a warning against violence against the LGBTQ community, particularly Transgender women, and ordered same-sex couples to be granted the right to marry per the Court's order. A similar law governing same-sex adoption was enacted in 2016.

South Korea

There is no official data available on the Transgender population in South Korea.

South Korean national law does not protect Transgender people from discrimination nor prohibits hate crimes based on sexual orientation or gender identity. The South Korean Constitution forbids discrimination based on gender, religion, or social status. The term "social status" includes Transgender people, according to the Ministry of Justice. However, there are no remedies for discrimination victims, and these "protections" are not enforced. According to Article 11 of the South Korean constitution, "There shall be no discrimination in political, economic, social, or cultural life on the basis of gender, religion, or social status." Conservatives and religious groups, however, argue that this equality was never intended to include same-sex marriage.

Russia

There is no official data available on the Transgender population. Wambui (2023) says, as for Transgender rights, it became possible to change the legal gender on identity documents in 1997. In 2018, this process was simplified significantly, permitting the change of legal gender based on a medical certificate without the need for surgery or hormone replacement therapy. These are among the few positive legal changes that have taken place in Russia concerning the community. The Russian Constitution has prohibited same-sex unions since 2020. Nobody can deny that Russia has become a notorious promoter of 'traditional values' and a denier of gender norms and rights at this point (Buyantueva, 2023). There is no explicit legal protection against sexual orientation and gender identity discrimination. Russia's conservative turn

Saudi Arabia

Saudi Arabia's government does not recognise Transgender rights. Saudi Arabia's criminal code is based on Islamic Sharia. Being Transgender is widely regarded as immoral and indecent, and the law punishes homosexual acts with the death penalty, up to life imprisonment, fines, deportation, Etc. During investigations and detentions, beatings and torture have been used. There is community violence against LGBT people. Under strict cyber laws, being openly gay or defying gender roles online can have severe implications. There was a case of three LGBT influencers who have been arrested in Saudi Arabia since 2019.

South Africa

Transgender people can use the Alteration of Sex Description and Sex Status Act 49 of 2003 to change their sex description in the birth register (South Africa, 2017). "Any person whose sexual characteristics have been altered by surgical or medical treatment, or by (SAFLII, 2022) evolution through natural development resulting in gender reassignment, or any person who is intersexed, may apply to the Director-General of the National Department of Home Affairs for the alteration of the sex description on his or her birth register (Government Gazette: Republic of South Africa, 2004, p.30)," Section 2(1) states.

Turkey

Transgender people face legal challenges, even though Turkey's LGBT rights are considered relatively progressive compared to most Muslim-majority countries.

This may seem surprising in a country where Transgender women ran for parliamentary office in 2015. Transgender rights and homosexuality have been legal since 1923, when modern Turkey was founded. However, some somewhat ambiguous prohibitions in the criminal code on "offences against public morality" can and have been interpreted to be used against the LGBT community. Furthermore, homosexuals are barred from serving in the military. Although homosexuality is technically legal in Turkey, life as a member of the LGBT community can be extremely difficult. According to a 2008 Human Rights Watch report, gay and Transgender communities face daily threats of violence and discrimination. It also emphasised the authorities and police's lack of response. A conservative anti-LGBTQ group marches in Istanbul to defend what they describe as traditional family values in the largest demonstration of its kind in Turkey.

United Kingdom

For the first time in the Census for England and Wales, Transgender and non-binary people were counted, revealing that 262,000 people identify as a gender other than their registered sex at birth. London is the most ethnically diverse region in England and Wales.

Transgender individuals have had the option to change their legal gender in the U.K. since April 2005, thanks to the Gender Recognition Act 2004. A Gender Recognition Panel, which evaluates the case and issues a Gender Recognition Certificate (GRC) after considering the evidence presented by the Transgender person, must have been the recipient of the GRC for two years. Sex reassignment surgery is not necessary for it to have occurred. The procedure outlined in the Gender Recognition Act of 2004 was ranked as one of the worst in Europe with "intrusive medical requirements" in a report released by the European Commission in June 2020, which means it now falls short of global human rights standards.

USA

According to a recent Pew Research Centre survey, 1.6% of U.S. adults are Transgender or nonbinary, meaning their gender differs from the sex they were assigned at birth. This finding comes as Transgender and nonbinary Americans become more visible in the media and to the general public.

The rights of Transgender people in the United States vary greatly depending on the jurisdiction. To promote the rights of Transgender, a coordinated national campaign has been launched. Anti-LGBTQ bills were introduced in 2021, and 80% of them sought to limit the rights of Transgender people expressly. When Transitioning their gender, Transgender people frequently ask for legal recognition of a name change. State by state, different laws apply to name changes. Transgender people may change their names in some states, provided the change does not enable fraud or criminal intent. The procedure may be more challenging in other states and require a court order or statute. The rules, which have drawn criticism for violating people's right to privacy and possibly exposing Transgender people to targeted hate crimes, may require an applicant to publish legal notices in newspapers to announce the name change.

Reference

Amnesty International UK. (2017, October 20). *What is the Universal Declaration of Human Rights?* Retrieved April 23, 2023, from https://www.amnesty.org.uk/universal-declaration-human-rights-UDHR

Analysis of the responses to the Gender Recognition Act (2004) consultation" (gov.uk)

Australian Bureau of Statistics. (2018). *2071.0 – Census of Population and Housing: Reflecting Australia – Stories from the Census, 2016*. https://www.abs.gov.au/ausstats/abs@.nsf/mf/2071.0. Retrieved April 23, 2023,

Bareque, A. (2023, April 18). *A bolt for a bolt, a nut for a nut?* LinkedIn. Retrieved April 23, 2023, from https://www.linkedin.com/pulse/bolt-nut-abdul-bareque/

Bearak M. & Cameron D. (June 16, 2016) *Analysis: Here are the 10 countries where homosexuality may be punished by death*. (Washington Post)

Buyantueva, R. (2023, February 21). *A history of LGBTQ rights in modern Russia: From progress to despair*. EUROPP. Retrieved April 23, 2023, from https://blogs.lse.ac.uk/europpblog/2023/02/21/a-history-of-lgbtq-rights-in-modern-russia-from-progress-to-despair/

Chan S. (October 21, 2009) Name Change Ruling" (The New York Times)

Chen, S. (2018, June 4). *China's complicated LGBT movement*. The Diplomat – The Diplomat is a current-affairs magazine for the Asia-Pacific, with news and analysis on politics, security, business, technology and life across the region. Retrieved April 23, 2023, from https://thediplomat.com/2018/06/chinas-complicated-lgbt-movement/

Corbitt T. (April 13, 2023) *American Civil Liberties Union* (https://www.aclu.org/cases/corbitt-v-taylor)

Elias C. (2022). *Laws for the Support of Transgenders in Argentina and Brazil*, (Roger Williams University)

Fadeke B., (March 23, 2023). *5 Human Rights Trans Activists Are Still Fighting for Around the World*. Global Citizen.

FashionUnited. (2019, July 25). *Q&A about M/ W/ D – German gender regulations*. Retrieved April 23, 2023, from https://fashionunited.info/news/business/q-a-about-m-w-d-german-gender-regulations/20190725147

Fico B. (April 27, 2018) *Brazil's Landmark Decision on Transgender Persons' Official Documents* (Oxford Human Rights Hub)

Flippo, Hyde (1996) *The Germany Way* (McGraw-Hill)

Ghoshal N. & Knight K. (2016) *Rights in Transition: Making Legal Recognition for Transgender People a Global Priority* (Human Rights Watch)

Giovanna M. & Wiedemann C. (November 28, 2017) Italy from Europe Published online by (Cambridge University Press)

Government Gazette: Republic of South Africa. (2004, March). *No. 49 of 2003: Alteration of Sex Description and Sex Status Act, 2003*. South African Government. Retrieved April 23, 2023, from https://www.gov.za/sites/default/files/gcis_document/201409/a49-03.pdf

Government of Canada. (2022, August 26). *The human rights of lesbian, gay, bisexual, Transgender, queer, 2-spirit and intersex persons*. GAC. Retrieved April 23, 2023, from https://www.international.gc.ca/world-monde/issues_development-enjeux_developpement/human_rights-droits_homme/rights_lgbti-droits_lgbti.aspx?lang=eng

H., Kyoko (2018). "Can human rights of a sexual minority in Japan be Guaranteed? A Comparison with Taiwan's efforts for Gender Equality." *Journal of Asian Women's Studies; Kitakyushu* Vol. 24, (Mar 2018): 1-23.

Heritage, C. (2022, May 16). *Rights of LGBTI persons*. Canada.ca. Retrieved April 23, 2023, from https://www.canada.ca/en/canadian-heritage/services/rights-lgbti-persons.html

Human Rights Watch. (2021, April 23). *Country profiles: Sexual orientation and gender identity*. Retrieved April 23, 2023, from https://www.hrw.org/video-photos/interactive/2021/04/23/country-profiles-sexual-orientation-and-gender-identity

Human Rights Watch. (2023). *Indonesia*. Human Rights Watch | Defending Human Rights Worldwide. Retrieved April 23, 2023, from https://www.hrw.org/asia/indonesia

J.P. (2017, June 5). *Chinese attitudes towards gay rights*. The Economist. Retrieved April 23, 2023, from https://www.economist.com/the-economist-explains/2017/06/05/chinese-attitudes-towards-gay-rights

Kyodo. (2021, November 9). "Transgender man in Japan wants switch recognised without surgery." *The Japan Times*. Retrieved April 23, 2023, from https://

www.japantimes.co.jp/news/2021/10/04/national/crime-legal/Transgender-man-japan-recognition/

LGBT Rights in Bulgaria. (2023). DBpedia. Retrieved April 23, 2023, from https://dbpedia.org/page/LGBT_rights_in_Bulgaria

Liza T. (January 6, 2023) U.K. Says 262,000 People Identified as Transgender in Census (Bloomberg)

M., Michael (12 December 2022). *South Korea's LGBTQ community confronts crushing headwinds in fight for equality* (nbcnews.com)

M4BL. (2021, January 28). *End the war on Black Trans, queer, gender nonconforming and intersex people.* Retrieved April 23, 2023, from https://m4bl.org/policy-platforms/end-the-war-Trans/

McAvan, E. (2016, August 11). *Why Australia's gender recognition laws need to change.* Topics. Retrieved April 23, 2023, from https://www.sbs.com.au/topics/pride/agenda/article/2016/08/11/why-australias-gender-recognition-laws-need-change

MENA Report. 2023. "India : 100th G20 Meeting During Indias G20 Presidency," April 18, 2023.

MENA Report. 2023. "India : Second G20 Sherpas Meeting in Kumarakom, Kerala (March 30 to April 2, 2023)," March 30, 2023.

Mendos L. R. (2020) State-Sponsored Homophobia 2020: Global Legislation Overview Update. (Geneva: ILGA World).

Peterson, E. (n.d.). *Lesbian, Gay, Bisexual, Transgender, and Questioning (LGBTQ) Youth.* Nationalsafeplace. Retrieved April 23, 2023, from https://www.nationalsafeplace.org/lgbtq

Pinheiro, E. (2022, January 24). *Brazil continues to be the country with the largest number of Trans people killed.* Pulitzer Center. Retrieved April 23, 2023, from https://pulitzercenter.org/stories/brazil-continues-be-country-largest-number-Trans-people-killed

Queen's University. (2023). *Definitions | Inclusive Queen's | Queen's University.* Queen's University Canada. Retrieved April 23, 2023, from https://www.queensu.ca/inclusive/initiatives/student-experiences-survey/definitions

Radzhana B. (February 21, 2023) *A history of LGBTQ rights in modern Russia: From progress to despair* (https://blogs.lse.ac.uk/)

SAFLII. (2022, October). *Alteration of sex description and sex status act 2003.* SAFLII SAFLII. Retrieved April 23, 2023, from https://www.saflii.org/za/legis/consol_act/aosdassa2003466/

South Africa. (2017). *Transgender Rights in South Africa.* Southern Africa Litigation Centre. Retrieved April 23, 2023, from https://www.southernafricalitigationcentre.org/wp-content/uploads/2017/08/Transgender-rights-in-South-Africa.pdf

Ummah N., Najeh M., and Tongat (July 1, 2020) *Transgender in Indonesia According to The Legal,* Health and Culture Perspective (ICILS)

UNDP. (2018). *Legal gender recognition in China: A legal and policy review | United Nations development programme.* Retrieved April 23, 2023, from https://www.undp.org/china/publications/legal-gender-recognition-china-legal-and-policy-review#:~:text=The%20Legal%20Gender%20Recognition%20in,gender%20recognition%20for%20Transgender%20people

United Nations. (2023). *The struggle of Trans and gender-diverse persons.* OHCHR. Retrieved April 23, 2023, from https://www.ohchr.org/en/special-procedures/ie-sexual-orientation-and-gender-identity/struggle-Trans-and-gender-diverse-persons

Wambui, P. (2023, March 5). *Putin – The West is normalising pedophilia by legalising homosexuality.* Mpasho. Retrieved April 23, 2023, from https://mpasho.co.ke/news/2023-03-05-putin--the-west-is-normalising-pedophilia-by-legalising-homosexuality/

Wharton J. (April 27, 2019*). Five men beheaded by Saudi Arabia were gay in claims from 'tortured confession* (Metro).

Widianto S. (January 11, 2023) *Indonesia's Transgender community fears threat posed by new law* (Reuters)

Wikipedia. (2023, April 20). *LGBT rights in France.* Wikipedia, the free encyclopedia. Retrieved April 23, 2023, from https://en.wikipedia.org/wiki/LGBT_rights_in_France

WONG, K. (2021, October 4). *Breaking down China's Transgender barriers.* Nikkei Asia. Retrieved April 23, 2023, from https://asia.nikkei.com/Life-Arts/Life/Breaking-down-China-s-Transgender-barriers

Wurthmann, L. C. (2023). "The German Transgender self-determination law: Explanatory factors for support within the population." *European Journal of Politics and Gender*, 1-5. https://doi.org/10.1332/251510821x16702343170849

CHAPTER 9

"I am Tyler, a Transgender Man!" Understanding the Gendered Self through the Video Game "TELL ME WHY"

Satyabrata Sahoo

This chapter critically inquiries about the gendered self within the video game "TELL ME WHY." The narrative revolves around twin brothers and sisters (Tyler and Alyson) Investigating their mother's death through the lens of their memories and childhood trauma. Through this game, not only did I try to understand the gender representation and interpretation of a Transitioning body (by analysing the game critically through formal game analysis), but also, to psychoanalyse myself to understand the emotions and virtues of a Transitioning body. At last, I tried to understand how society involves and affects a Transitioning body and how does a Transitioned body affect the community. Overall, this chapter revolves around the Transition of self, parents, family, society and how they affect one another through this game.

> "Gender Representation and interpretation in video games provide us a vivid imagination to do gender in different perspectives."
>
> Malkowski And Russworm (2017)

Introduction

To understand the virtues of gender representation in video games, we have to understand gender representation, its importance and the ways of imagining it. Gender representation is a phenomenon in which gender and its functionality are shown. Gender and its roles, when expressed through its representative approach in media, we observe a binary notion of presenting a gender that is often associated with the biological sex of a person (Butler 1990, 1993)

(Popa, Gavriliu 2015). We never see gender as a social construct that has a set of behavioural patterns. So, with these virtues of social norms, one can see that the representation of a body is either masculine or feminine i.e., a set of behavior and qualities that are associated with a male or female. For example, I am male which means it talks about my biologically assigned gender. But I like blue T-shirts which denote gender construct which talks about the preference of certain sexually oriented people. It symbolises masculine nature but can be worn by both males and females. This construct is irrelevant in a present society where there is a gender-fluid, non-binary approach to gender and sexuality of more than seventy types. For example, when we see a Transgender flag, it has both pink (as a feminine feature) and blue (as a masculine feature) stripes. It means a body can traverse through masculine and feminine features as per self-perception.

Gender representation, when studied through video games redirects the imagination of seeing gender differently (MALKOWSKI 2017). The protagonists in RPGs (Role Playing Games), the NPCs (Non-Playable characters), the artwork in the game, and the collectibles present within the game always define gender representation in a unique way. For example, in a game, the non-playable character is portrayed as a male, a warrior but wears female armor. All other characters in Warrior are males and wear male armor. Seeing this particular character, we imagine the world of cross-dressers and question the normalised gender roles and responsibilities. So, through video games one can question gender representation, subverting the roles and identities carried by gender and finally questioning the self about their preferences. To understand this phenomenon in a better way, I have played and viewed critically, the first Transgender-themed video game "TELL ME WHY". This game not only inquiries about the Transgender themselves but also sees and questions the social norms, and values of the cis-normative society and the struggle faced by non-binary people within their communities.

Traversing through the story

TELL ME WHY – is an episodic story-styled game developed by Dontnod Entertainment studio for Xbox One. The story consists of three episodes that follow up the quest of investigating the death of the protagonist's (twin brother and sister; Tyler and Alyson) mother.

The study follows up the ludo-narratological way as the main questions about Transgenders' life can be answered through the ludic element of the game or the narratological element of the game. The whole game is studied under formal game analysis (Björk and Lankoski, 2015) and closely observed (Gray 2010) to analyse the story and the narrative that the video game offers. I critically analysed the Transition of the Transgender character, psychoanalysed myself, recorded my experiences and described my thoughts through thick descriptions (Boyd and Crawford 2011) where I shared my thoughts and experiences. I have also taken some screenshots and collected the collectibles to analyse the game in a holistic way using Calleja's (2007) six-point framework. Following up I have summarised the whole game:

IMAGE I – Showing the post of the Game "TELL ME WHY"

Source: https://www.tellmewhygame.com/

Chapter 1: Homecoming

The game opens with a flashback showing Tyler's admission to the homicide of his mom, Mary-Ann, justifiably as a kid in 2005. Tyler, now an adult, leaves the juvenile detention facility (Fireweed Residential Centre) to which he was sentenced ten years earlier and reunites with Alyson, who has been adopted by Eddy, the incident's investigating officer. The twins return to Delos Crossing to sell their childhood home with the intention of moving on, but despite the efforts of Mary-Ann's friend and housekeeper Sam, who had turned to alcoholism after her death, the house is in disrepair. While exploring the house, the twins recall fond childhood memories, particularly fairy tales told by their mother about a runaway princess and her two goblin companions, which she compiled into an illustrated journal known as the "Book of Goblins." They also discovered that their mom is trying to understand Tyler by studying "Raising a Transgender child" which completely shocked them. The twins then visit Tessa at her store, where they learn about Mary-Ann's behavior which became increasingly odd and eccentric shortly before she died, and they learn about Tessa's discussions with Mary-Ann about Tyler's gender identity. Then at the Delos police station, the twins later speak with Eddy, but he denies their request to view her file. Alyson later encounters a flashback where she wounded Mary-Ann with a scissor, and starts to experience the ill effects of post-horrible pressure.

IMAGE II – Tyler experiencing his freedom after spending ten years in Juvenile Detention Centre Source: https://youtu.be/IDq0uWp7nek

MAGE III – Stories in Book of Goblin Source: https://youtu.be/IDq0uWp7nek

Chapter 2: Family Secrets

The files concerning Mary-Ann are discovered when the twins break into the police archive the following morning. They discovered that their mother died due to drowning and also discovered Tessa's plan. Eddy admits that he had gone to Mary-Ann to warn her about Tessa's plan (of sending the twins to social services) after learning about their break-in and he was also apologetic to send Tyler to the Detention center. Tessa justifies her actions by claiming that Mary-Ann is isolating herself from the community and that her alleged mental instability and parental incompetence are putting her children in danger. The twins confront Tessa. When the twins get back to the house, they find the barn is on fire and an arsonist running away from the scene. The twins discovered, after putting out the fire, that the arsonist had tried to get into a locked box beneath the barn floor. Inside the box, they found letters from someone telling Mary-Ann to get an abortion. Later, the twins recall Mary-Ann arguing with an unidentified man on a boat. Following a disagreement, the twins briefly separate.

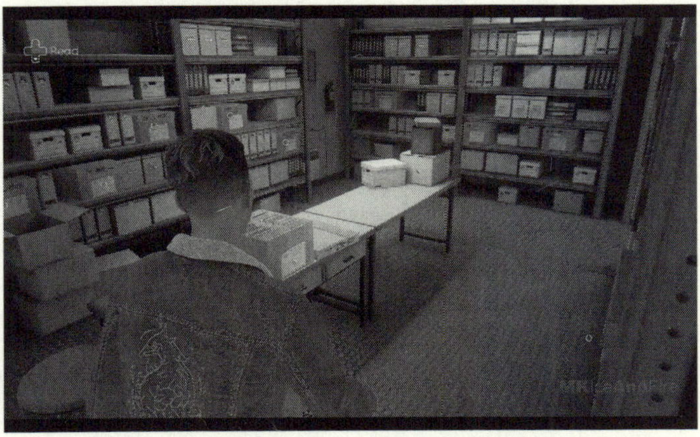

IMAGE IV – Tyler Investigating Mary-Ann's Death

Source: https://youtu.be/gDThXo9rg48

Chapter 3: Inheritance

Alyson's mental health deteriorates as a result of feeling guilty and anxious about Mary-Ann's death, which causes a severe panic attack. Alyson visits Sam after she recovers to inquire about their possible familial ties. However, she learns that an old photograph in his possession shows a hidden loft above the barn. Using the Book of

Goblins, the twins reunite to investigate the loft and discover a room filled with intricate puzzles. They learn that the fairy tales Mary-Ann told were actually metaphors for her troubled past: brought into the world to a domineering family, she fell pregnant and escaped to Delos Crossing to bring up her child, a child named Leo, who didn't make due. The twins track down an image of their late half-kin, alongside a letter from Mary-Ann which is addressed to them. The twins understand that Mary-Ann had experienced a psychological episode over her feeling of dread toward social administrations removing her enduring youngsters. The twins come to the conclusion that Tom Vecchi, Tessa's husband, was the unidentified man on the boat – their biological father. The player Alyson must decide after the twins confront Tom, whether she thinks Mary-Ann planned to kill herself and her two children or only herself when Tyler interrupted her (as Tom claims). Whatever the choices maybe but in the end, they sold their mother's house and both of them moved to Juneau (a city in Alaska) to start their new life.

IMAGE V – Alyson finds out about the hidden loft Source: https://youtu.be/2hm1G1HNEWo

IMAGE VI – The twins Alyson and Tyler explore the hidden loft to find out the secret of their mother Source: https://youtu.be/2hm1G1HNEWo

Understanding the Transition of the character and channelising my thought through psychoanalysis

Studying the video game "Tell Me Why" through Formal Game analysis has given me the perspectives to critically understand Why did Tyler feel that his mother Mary-Ann tried to kill him during his Transition? Why did Tyler take the blame of his mother on himself? Why do we see a defensiveness towards society within Tyler? Why does Tyler see the memories in a descriptive way?

The society presented within the two timelines i.e., 2005 and 2015 are very different. In 2005, the people of Delos Crossing saw gender Transition as social deviance and tried to correct them while in 2015 people are fairly accepting of Transgender people. To understand why Tyler sees his mother as a killer we have to understand her idea for her daughter and her socialisation process. Growing up in a cis-normative society the very idea of boyhood within a girl is not accepted by his mother. She never allows Tyler to cut his hair or to join the hockey team rather she scolds and says no to everything. Tessa, one of her friends, suggested sending Tyler to a conversion therapy camp. Mary-Ann tries to protect Ollie (later Transitioned to Tyler) from being transitioned. Seeing Shotgun in her mother's hand on the day of his haircut, Tyler builds up the perspective that his mother is willing to hurt him to keep him away from Transition.

IMAGE VII – Poster Showing Trans Visibility Day Source: https://youtu.be/IDq0uWp7nek

Unfortunately, Mary-Ann died due to drowning after being stabbed with a scissor by Alyson, his twin sister and fell into the lake. The Police Chief knew about the autopsy report (death due to drowning) but he preferred to send Tyler to the Centre for Troubled Youth (Fireweed Recreation and residential center i.e., a juvenile detention center) to help him with his Transition. But we can see that Tyler was also interested in going to the center and took the blame for murdering his mother on himself for murdering her mother. This shows his brotherly nature of taking family responsibility i.e., saving his sister from trouble. Moreover, he already knew that in order to become a Transgender male he will have to shut away the people from the society he lived in at that moment and seek some help from mentors and counsellors to identify himself. Moreover, staying in the center helped him to be a mentor himself. We can see that he had not seen his sister for the last ten years as he was undergoing a series of Transition processes and testosterone treatments to change himself into a man completely. He doesn't want to let her sister know about his masculine changes like the beard, the acne, etc. So, it created a defensiveness we can see in man, to endure pain, to take responsibility.

IMAGE VIII – The calendar of Tyler's Testosterone Intakes Source: https://youtu.be/IDq0uWp7nek

Transitioning people have the souls of either a male or a female; thus, Transitioning to their masculine and feminine self subsequently in following times. For Tyler, his Transition process is a pool of emotions and trauma that reflects his past. Thus, certain places, certain music and certain situations trigger memories of the past. As author of this chapter and viewer of this game, and a patient with

Borderline Personality disorder, I also feel a sudden flow of memories by listening to these following words:

IMAGE IX – Tyler experiencing his past memories.

Source: https://youtu.be/IDq0uWp7nek

> "Tyler – Whoa! I just got hit with a flood of Memories. Do you see what i am seeing, Alyson?
>
> Alyson – Yeah!........... It doesn't matter that they don't believe us…… It doesn't matter that they kept us apart……. it doesn't matter that finding the truth feels impossible……. the only thing that matters is you're my brother and the only way to move forward is to keep looking back.
>
> Tyler – We've been getting these visions whenever we see or hear something really emotional. Everything we thought we knew about Mary-Ann just got thrown out the window. I thought coming here would be closing a chapter of our lives….."

These words particularly hit my mind to understand what it means to be Transgender and uncover your unseen history. The worst nightmares suddenly come in front of us which will change our perceptions of certain things. So, through psychoanalysing myself or the psychoanalysis of self (Leffert, 2023) I tried to understand why I am so interested in this game. What does it mean to have those memories and emotional outbursts during the Transition? Why do Transitioning people socially seclude themselves? Why do they prefer to write and compile their thoughts? Why do they love to be with nature, not around people? At last I want to explore about my feelings about "the Transition in a body."

At first, due to the immersive experience, I see myself as the Transman protagonist Tyler. The game in itself narrates the conceptualised experiences of gender Transition. Moreover, the character Transition of the protagonist Tyler from Introvert to Ambivert recreates my personality. Sometimes I feel like this is one way or another my story, my journey/Transition from cisgender to gender-fluidity. Talking about memories and emotional outbursts, there are a lot of bad memories due to the prejudicial mindset and concepts of cis-normative society. In fact, these memories add up in our minds and create an imaginary world that instigates a sense of panic and emotional outbursts which is quite discomforting and painful. So, to endure their discomforts we socially seclude ourselves and through those discomforts, they try to understand their stance on their identity. During seclusion, they ask themselves certain questions about their identity, preferences, choices, feelings, thoughts, minds, etc. They jot down these ideas to understand the question about themselves like who am I? Why am I like this? This seclusion enhances the capability to face the world with their new identity, a kind of Metamorphosis we see in nature; from a caterpillar to a butterfly. These thoughts of these butterflies' kind of take us away from the people to the forest or nature where we can listen to our inner selves by bonding with nature – to feel the leaves of novice, to feel the water of memories, to feel the air of freedom. From a gender non-binary ness, we reimagine this world where we want to live – Away from civilisation, embracing nature, delving into the world of books and writing our story.

In other words, this game really helped me to understand myself and my approach towards my Transition process to gender fluid. Every time, it is so confusing that I can't understand what is imagination and what is reality! Everything imaginary becomes real and everything real becomes imaginary. Through this game, I can see that how everybody tried to hurt me, bullied me for being different but this very nature of differences paved a new way to understand myself and evolve my thoughts. I have had been frightened and still confused about everything, about my gender and my identity, but the character of Tyler in this game helped me to understand that change in one's choices are natural and one should embrace it. I want to run away from this society to a desolated place with minimal civilisational interaction like Tyler did in this game, I want to groom myself and change myself in desolation like Tyler did in this game but I also want to explore more about myself, write about myself to ideate a new world beyond cis normativity, as it should be where everyone is equal and has the equal right to follow anything religion, gender, sexuality, philosophical approaches. No Boundaries for your dreams. Only explore me in myself – my ideas to see future of humanity.

IMAGE X – The diary of Ollie (Tyler's name before Transition) Source: https://youtu.be/IDq0uWp7nek

Beyond Transgender: thoughts of the Game

This game not only inquiries about Transgender(s) themselves, but it also inquiries about the bigger picture of how parents see this Transition. How do parents feel about the Transition of their child? How does society see these Transitions? How and why does society try to control these Transitions? Through this game, Mary-Ann (despite having her past traumas about running away from her parents to start a new life, the miscarriage before the twins and marital affairs) does not wish to agree with her daughter Ollie's Transition to male (later known as Tyler in the game) she was completely resisting the gender Transitioning within her daughter. But later on, she tried to understand the Transitioning process and started inquiring about "raising your Transgender child". She was loving her child so much that the news of her child being taken away by the social service almost broke her heart as her daughters were everything to her – her happiness, her life in her traumatised past of having a miscarriage and her affairs with Tessa's husband – Tom. But she never showed her concern to her daughter Ollie that she accepts her the way she is. Rather Tyler's haircut and the shotgun in her hand created a misconception and traumatised Tyler (Transitioned Ollie); to believe that his mother follows the idea of cis-normative traditional families. He feels like she will kill him to stop him from Transitioning from a girl to a boy. The society in which we live never understands this kind of gender Transition. They see it more like social deviance; a way to outright the social norms. And society mostly pushes these Transitioning people towards the cis-normative social order, such as marriage with a cisgender, sending them to religious centres to stop their Transition, and sometimes conversion therapy to brainwash their questions on identities. In this game when Tessa (Mary-Ann's friend) knew about Tyler's problem with Transition, she didn't want to make Mary-Ann understand that this Transition is normal but rather tried to convince her to send Tyler to Virtue Seeker Youth Camp for conversion therapy.

IMAGE XI – Alyson showing Tyler their mother's dilemma Source: ***https://youtu.be/IDq0uWp7nek***

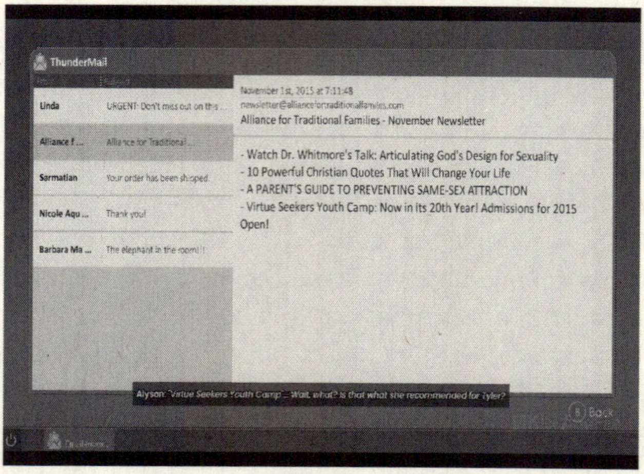

IMAGE XII – Alyson discovered Tessa's recommendation about Tyler Source: https://youtu.be/IDq0uWp7nek

Conclusion

The Transition of gender is seldom lone rather accompanies a bigger picture of social exclusion, parental dilemma, mental health, past traumas, introversion and much more. But bringing all of this to a picture and figuring out the problems to move forward, is a whole new thing. Transgender minds really fascinate me, and motivate me to understand on a whole new level through this game. This game purely revolves around Marshall McLuhan's idea on media in his book Understanding Media: The Extension of Man (2015) where he explains media as propagation to channel and present it in a way the society perceives certain ideas – the thoughts of the human mind, the imagination within the mind, social prejudices, the dilemma of taking a stand for yourself and the ability to self-question. So, through this game, I see an extension of a Transgender's mind, the dilemma of a mother and society on Transgender identities, and the mental peculiarities of society on the Transgender perspectives.

References

Boyd, D. and Crawford, K., 2011. "Six provocations for big data." In: Oxford Internet Institute, *A decade in internet time: Symposium on the dynamics of the internet and society*. Oxford, 21 September 2011.

Butler, J. (1990). *Gender trouble: Feminism and the subversion of identity*. New York: Routledge.

Butler, J. (1993). *Bodies that matter: On the discursive limits of sex*. New York: Routledge.

Calleja, G., 2007. D*igital game involvement: A conceptual model. Games and Culture*, 2(3), 236-260

Garcia, J. (2021, February 11). *Tell me why review. IGN*. Retrieved April 13, 2023, from https://www.ign.com/articles/tell-me-why-review

Gray, J., 2010. *Show sold separately: Promos, spoilers, and other media paratexts*. New York: NYU Press.

Henley, S. (2020, September 10). Tell me why review: "The new gold standard for Trans characters in games". Games radar. Retrieved April 13, 2023, from https://www.gamesradar.com/tell-me-why-review/

Koch, C. (2021, June 1). *Tell me why is free so players can support Trans and queer communities directly*. Game Spot. Retrieved April 13, 2023, from https://www.gamespot.com/articles/tell-me-why-is-free-so-players-can-support- Trans-and-queer-communities-directly/1100-6492231/

L. Doornkamp, S. Groeneveld, M. G. Groeneveld, L. D. Van der Pol & J. Mesman (2022). "Understanding the Symbolic Effects of Gender Representation: A Multi – Source Study in Education," *International Public Management Journal*, DOI: 10.1080/10967494.2021.1991534

Lankoski, P. and Björk, S., 2015. "Formal analysis of gameplay." In: Lankoski, P. and Björk, S., eds. *Game Research Methods: An overview*. Pittsburgh: ETC Press, 23- 35.

Leffert, M. (2023). "So Why Do We Need Philosophy Anyway? Phenomenology, Postmodernism, and the Plague in the Psychoanalytic Workplace." In Psychoanalysis, *the self and the world: Postphenomenology, Consciousness, and death* (pp. 17–52). Chapter, Routledge, Taylor & Francis Group.

Malkowski, J. (2017). "I Turned Out To Be Such A Damsel In Distress": Noir Games and the Unrealised Femme Fatale. In J. Malkowski & T. M. Russworm (Eds.), *Gaming Representation: Race, Gender, and Sexuality in Video Games* (pp. 19–37). Indiana University Press. https://doi.org /10.2307/j.ctt2005rgq.6

Malkowski, J., & Russworm, T. M. (2017). "Introduction: Identity, Representation, and Video Game Studies beyond the Politics of the Image." In J. Malkowski & T. M. Russworm (Eds.), *Gaming Representation: Race, Gender, and Sexuality in Video Games* (pp. 1–16). Indiana University Press. https://doi.org/ 10.2307/j.ctt2005rgq.5

McLuhan, M., & Gordon, W. T. (2015). *Understanding media: The extensions of man.* Gingko Press.

Popa, D., & Gavriliu, D. (2015). *Gender representations and Digital Media. Procedia – Social and Behavioral Sciences*, 180, 1199–1206. https://doi.org/10.1016/ j.sbspro.2015.02.244

Ruberg, B. (2017). "Playing To Lose: The Queer Art of Failing at Video Games." In J. Malkowski & T. M. Russworm (Eds.), *Gaming Representation: Race, Gender, and Sexuality in Video Games* (pp. 197–211). Indiana University Press. https://doi.org/10.2307/j.ctt2005rgq.16

CHAPTER 10

Transgender Representation in Mainstream Media

Aditi Dubey

Transgenders have been a part of society since ancient times, however after British colonisation, people started to view Transgenders as a bad influence on people and children. They still are socially outcasted from society. Several laws have been passed to protect the rights of Transgenders in India. It is important for us to include them in society and to make them feel seen. Therefore, representation is important. This paper aims to show the ways in which Transgenders have been impacted by negative portrayal. For over two decades, Transgenders have been forced to perceive themselves negatively. In this research paper, examples have been given of movies showing Transgenders in a negative light.

Introduction

Before I begin with this research paper, understanding the term, 'Transgender' is necessary. According to Mitchell (2019), Transgender refers to a person whose gender identity is different from the one the person is assigned with birth. Transgender is an umbrella term. It includes Trans women and Trans men. After COVID-19 hit, the media has become very pervasive. Almost everyone uses at least one social media platform to stay connected with society. People during their idle time choose to watch movies and shows. Subsequently they get influenced by the movies and shows characters. The way directors portray characters, especially Trans characters in movies is very important. People get easily influenced by characters in shows and movies. There can be bad as well as good influence, but it is observed that the way Trans characters are portrayed are in bad light. They are either portrayed as psychotic serial killers or a comic-relief. This paper will aim to show that Transgenders have been impacted when portrayed in movies and shows. Most importantly, I aim to make cisgender people realise that making a mockery out of a large group of people isn't right and it isn't justified.

Transgender Representation in Mythologies and Folklores

India is the world's largest democracy with over 9.12 crore eligible voters, it is the 6th largest economy with a robust network of national highways (Times Of India) What this fails to mention is that India ranks 132 out of a total of 191 countries according to United Nations Development Programme (UNDP) in Human Development Index. According to Bradley & Halbrook (2022) UNDP measures HDI in terms of a long and healthy life, education and a decent standard of living. This is a let down for India as its rank has fallen by two places since last year i.e. 2020-21. So, despite India's robust growth in the economic and medical sector, it is lacking in terms of its progress socially. In spite of India recognising Transgenders as third gender, the first two being males and females in no chronological order. Transgenders face several hindrances socially and economically due to stereotypes and taboos. This statement might have been proved wrong before the British colonised India in the 16th century. Hindu mythology very implicitly yet vehemently mentions Transexualism and gender-fluid persons. The existence of Transgender community can be traced in earlier Hindu religious texts.

A few instances of Hindu mythology mentioning Transgenders can be found in the Puranas where *Mohini* is the female avatar of Vishnu. In the Ramayana, when Lord Rama was sent to exile for a period of 14 years in the forest, his devoted followers followed him to the forest but he insisted all men and women to return to Ayodhya. But, all Transgenders (*Hijra*s) stayed with him. This deeply impressed Lord Rama and he gave them power to confer their blessings on occasions like birthdays and marriage anniversaries. Another instance of a gender – fluid person in Hindu mythology is of *Arjuna* from Mahabharata who was anathematised by *Urvashi* that he would lose his masculinity if he rejected her advances. *Arjuna* further considered this curse a boon because he disguised himself as a dance teacher. He called himself *Brihnnala* during that period when *Pandavas* were sent to exile. This however got influenced rather negatively by the British.

During the colonial period, the British criminalised homosexuality i.e. they criminalised non-procreative sexual activities under Section 377 of the Indian Penal Code (Taneja, 2018). This was introduced with an aim to attack and target people involved in "natural" relationships. This law got partially repealed in 2019 and decriminalised homosexuality. What commoners tend to overlook is the fact that Transgenders, *Hijras*, were important people in the Mughal courts who had the responsibility and power of collecting taxes (Arondekar, 2018). The British colonised India for nearly 200 years and the implications of the laws and regulations they passed can be seen today in various countries of South-East Asia. British colonisation over South-East Asia more or less forced people to think of Transgenders as sinners even though India had been so open to Transexuality and gender fluidity. Blaming the British for the setback of Transgenders in a society is just and right. One of the first case laws which can be recalled is of Queen Empress v Khairati wherein a person in Moradabad was found crossdressing as well as singing and mingling with a group of women. This person called themselves Khaitari and was one of the first who was prosecuted under Section 377 of the Indian Penal Code (IPC).

Transgenders still face discrimination and are ostracised in India. This includes them not getting adequate medical treatment from government and private hospitals, feeling excluded, physical, sexual and mental violence. Transgenders weren't even protected until The Transgender Persons (Protection of Rights) Act was passed in 2019. This is a shameful situation for Indians and their law governing institutions. Transgenders weren't even lawfully recognised until the 2019 act was passed. Their situation has become progressively worse because of the ever growing negative stereotypes. Several Not-For-Profit organisations like Naz Foundation have worked towards Transgenders rights. They provide shelter, food and basic amenities for Transgenders. Despite Transgenders getting legally recognised, their rights still continue to get violated.

Representation makes people feel seen. People look for their real life stories in movies and shows. Watching movies that portray people's life stories can make people comfortable. However, movies that portray Transgenders in a good light does the opposite work for them. Transgenders are already suppressed and face discrimination in all fields of life. Watching themselves on screen doing out-of-box things and earning a living. This empowers Transgenders to work towards earning a living by breaking barriers. This practice often leads to them facing more suppression as conservatives think of them doing chores as a rebellious act. Influence can be good or bad and it is the producers and directors responsibility to do justice to the characters they are portraying in shows and movies.

Transgender Persons (Protection of Rights) Act, 2019 – Critical analysis

According to the nation-wide census held in India in 2011, the population of Transgenders is 4,87,803 with Uttar Pradesh having the majority population of 1,37,465 and Lakshadweep consisting of only 2 Transgenders. In India Transgenders are denied basic facilities and documentation that men and women are expected to have. In 2020, when COVID-19 hit, the government declared that Transgender persons would get Rs.1,500 as direct Transfer and ration supplies. Despite their population only a small number of Transgenders received direct Transfer and ration supplies. (India Spend, 2011)

Government failed to send them the amount insured as well as free ration because they lacked documentation. Transgenders lack documentation and don't have documents that contain their personal details because of the exclusion they face from society. No one except the society, us, should be blamed for the exclusion they continue to face. Social exclusion leads to several mental health issues such as anxiety, depression and them getting involved in illegal activities.

The Transgender Persons (Protection of Rights) Act commenced on 10th January, 2020. This bill claims to protect Transgenders identity and rights. However, right after this bill was tabled in Rajya Sabha on November 20, many people voiced their resentment during the Delhi Queer parade. This bill does in fact consist of some loopholes and it will end up hindering the rights of persons it once wanted to uphold. Firstly, according to this bill a Transgender person must apply to the district magistrate in order to get an identity which will set an indication of them being a 'Transgender'. This is contradictory to the NALSA judgment in which it was held that people can self-determine themselves as male, female or Transgenders. And they won't require a medical certificate or approval from the District Magistrate. This will force Transgenders to get gender reassignment surgery.

Secondly, getting documents from government offices in India is a tedious task. According to this bill, people who wish to recognise themselves as Transgenders must go sex reassignment surgery and the medical certificate must be examined by the District Magistrate. This will present a lot of hurdles related to bureaucracy that Transgenders must navigate through.

In 2018, when Section 377 of the Indian Penal Code was partially struck down, the Supreme Court recognised that Transgenders face discrimination and oppression at the hands of law enforcement officials. A lot of provisions under this act are in contradiction to the measures proposed under the NALSA judgment. This act does not provide reservation for Transgenders despite the NALSA judgment recognising Transgenders as socially and educationally backward class. Reservation for Transgenders in government offices and educational institutions is necessary and required as they can only be empowered through equity i.e. giving them a sort of incentive so that they can be at par with other men and women. It might seem impossible for Transgenders to be at par with men and women but this can be achieved through right people governing people and laws in India.

This bill nevertheless after 75 years of independence recognised Transgenders facing discrimination in healthcare, educational and employment institutions. It also provided two years of imprisonment for people who deny Transgenders access to public places. This doesn't change the fact that the government must listen to people who have been oppressed since time immemorial.

Transgender Representation in Movies and Shows

The representation of Transgenders in media, especially, in a positive limelight is important as movies have always been directed and produced for Cisgender public at large. Directors, historically, weren't sympathetic to Transgenders. In case directors wanted to show Transgenders in movies it was often in inappropriate ways. This genre was previously called 'cross dressing cinema' but now it is called 'Transgender Cinema'. Earlier in a lot of films, Transgenders were portrayed as psychotic serial killers or people who can't be trusted to live in a society. For instance, the movie 'Psycho' produced and directed by Alfred Hitchcock, shows Norman Bates as a pathological serial killer, this archetype continued in movies such as 'Silence of the Lambs', 'Freebie and the Bean' etc.

In several movies and shows, Transgenders are 'sexualised' and 'fetishisised'. Society hardly thinks of Transwomen as women, this forces them to sexualise themselves. They want to meet the beauty standards set for women by society. This hinders them changing at their own pace without any societal pressure. Directors of films place too much pressure on clothes, people playing Trans characters, the way they should act, the way they should do their makeup. For over two decades movies have shown the way people should perceive Trans people in real life and also the way Trans people perceive themselves. Women are already dehumanised by society and are forced to follow set beauty standards. Now, Trans women are fighting for their rights to be accepted by society.

This is specifically focusing on Transgender representation in Indian cinema. India produces a large number of movies and shows annually and directors have tried to show Transgender characters in movies. They are mostly portrayed as bizarre and grotesque characters. Trans characters in Indian cinema are shown mainly to show mockery. This practice has continued for so long that people rarely try to understand their struggles and discrimination they face. Trans characters in movies were more or less introduced only for mockery. For instance, Rishi Kapoor in Rafoo Chakkar.

As mentioned earlier, Transgenders are either showcased as psychotic serial killers or comic relief. In Sadak, a movie directed by Mahesh Bhatt shows a Trans woman named 'Maharani' as a serial killer who uses torturous methods to kill young women (Pause for Perspectives) This is nothing but reinforcing the stereotypes. This stigma can only be removed if directors are mindful of what they are portraying in movies and shows. As it impacts the society as a whole.

Cinema Showing Transgenders in a Positive Light

After decades of Transgenders being shown in a bad light, directors have begun to show real life struggles of Trans people. For instance, Disclosure (2020) is a documentary showing how Transgenders are misunderstood and one of the main reasons for that is misrepresentation of Trans people in cinema. Second, Boys Don't Cry (2000) is a movie based on real life, where Brandon Teena, a trangender teenager was sexually assaulted and murdered. This shows how Trans people are not accepted in society and get engaged in negative influence. Third, Paris Is Burning (1990) shows how glamorous New York is but it also touches upon homophobia, racism and Transphobia faced by people especially minorities.

Conclusion

Conclusion that can be drawn from this research paper is that the way in which the media portrays Transgenders is that it is unethical. One of the main reasons why directors and producers use Trans characters in movies and shows is monetary incentive. Directors misinterpret stories and struggles of Transgenders in movies. This leads to them facing discrimination in real life. Everyone wants to see their story on a screen and always being shown in a bad light can be demoralising. Media needs to be mindful of how they portray Transgenders. Thus, Bollywood as well as Hollywood must change their ways.

References

Bradley, N., & Halbrook, S. (2022). *Understanding GDP.* Home Comptroller. Texas.Gov. Retrieved April 22, 2023, from https://comptroller.texas.gov/economy/fiscal-notes/2022/feb/gdp.php

Fatima, I. (n.d.). *Media representation of Trans identities.* Pause for Perspective – Psychological Services for A Well-Lived Life. Retrieved April 22, 2023, from https://hyderabadpsychologist.com/media-representation-of-Trans-identities/

Hunter, S. (2019, June 17). *Hijrasand the legacy of British colonial rule in India.* Engenderings. Retrieved April 22, 2023, from https://blogs.lse.ac.uk/gender/2019/06/17/*Hijra*s-and-the-legacy-of-british-colonial-rule-in-india/

Mitchell, B. (2019, June 26). *How has the LGBT+ acronym evolved?* PinkNews | Latest lesbian, gay, bi and Trans news | LGBTQ+ news. Retrieved April 22, 2023, from https://www.thepinknews.com/2017/11/06/how-has-the-lgbt-acronym-evolved/

Olund, E. (2013). Geography written in lightning: Race, sexuality, and regulatory aesthetics in *The birth of a Nation. Annals of the Association of American Geographers, 103*(4), 925-943. https://doi.org/10.1080/00045608.2011.653738

Raman, S. (2021, June 11). *Denied visibility in official data, Transgender Indians can't access benefits, services.* IndiaSpend: Data journalism, analysis on Indian economy, education, healthcare, agriculture, politics. Retrieved April 22, 2023, from https://www.indiaspend.com/gendercheck/denied-visibility-in-official-data-millions-of-Transgender-indians-cant-access-benefits-services-754436

Schumer, L. (2022, November 22). *15 Transgender movies and documentaries to watch right now.* Good Housekeeping. Retrieved April 22, 2023, from https://www.goodhousekeeping.com/life/entertainment/g36107109/Trans-movies-documentaries/

Srinivasan, S., & Chandrasekaran, S. (2020). "Transsexualism in Hindu mythology." *Indian Journal of Endocrinology and Metabolism, 24*(3), 235. https://doi.org/10.4103/ijem.ijem_152_20

Taneja, R. (2018, January 8). *Section 377: All you need to know*. NDTV.com. Retrieved April 22, 2023, from https://www.ndtv.com/india-news/section-377-all-you-need-to-know-1797355

The Times of India. (2022, August 15). *75th Independence Day: India's journey since independence | India news – Times of India*. Retrieved April 22, 2023, from https://timesofindia.indiatimes.com/india/in-charts-indias-journey-since-independence/articleshow/93573389.cms

CHAPTER 11

Rights of LGBTQIA+ in India and their Struggle for Societal Acceptance

Aditi Mishra

This paper mainly focuses on the LGBTQIA+ community which includes Lesbians,Gays, Bisexuals, Homosexuals, Queers, Transgenders etc. along with their fundamental reserved rights and struggles. Even after decriminalising section 377 of the Indian penal code (In Navtej Singh Johar vs. Union of India) by the honorable Supreme Court of India, we as citizens haven't accepted them and their different sexual orientations. They are a socially marginalised community and have been subjected to Discrimination for ages because of societal unacceptance and our conservative approach toward their heteronormative behavior. Even their basic fundamental rights have been a matter of significant controversies and heated debates in and across India. The legal framework has undergone drastic changes, but we are yet to establish a society civilised enough to respect them and their rights. Even in the 21st century, we are lagging in achieving equality among all genders. Some developed countries have established laws for equal employment opportunities, public accommodations, marriage, and adoption. At the same time, others are facing high social backlash and unacceptance of their (LGBTQIA+) community, behavior, nature, and sexual orientations. The central government of India ought to realise that just making new laws for them won't help. Rather implementation of those laws in a real sense would be more helpful. The paper emphasises the daily challenges, hardships, and struggles faced by the LGBTQIA+ community and the fundamental rights reserved for them. They have faced many challenges over time. Some of them are discriminated based on gender, social stigma, and isolation, lack of legal recognition and support, sexual and emotional abuse, inadequate health care facilities, and many more unaddressed issues. The final analysis of this research paper would come up with some solutions and opinions for the betterment, upliftment, and well-being of the community.

Introduction

> "Love is not a sin, and God does not create mistakes." – Laverne Cox

It is crucial to keep in mind that members of the LGBTQ community come from a variety of ethnic groups, cultural traditions, religious affiliations, and socioeconomic backgrounds. It is crucial to establish a secure and welcoming workplace that recognises the complexity and diversity of the LGBTQ community. The LGBTQ community has made great progress towards attaining recognition and rights, including the legalisation of same-sex marriage in many nations and protections against discrimination. However, prejudice and bigotry still persist, and the community keeps pushing for more tolerance and understanding.

Definition of the term LGBTQIA+

The acronym LGBTQIA+ is explained as follows:

> "Lesbian" is a term used for a woman who is sexually attracted to another woman.

Likewise, the term "gay" is used for those men who are sexually attracted to another man. At the same time, this particular terminology is used as a reference to the whole LGBTQIA+ community as an umbrella term. Bisexual is a term used for all those individuals (men and women) who are attracted to another man, woman, or any other recognised gender. They have a wide range of sexual orientations.

Transgenders are such people who do not match their gender identity, or more specifically, those who have different behavioural, emotional, and sexual identities. Q: "Queer" is yet again an umbrella term that can be used broadly for all those mentioned above or for those who are yet to identify their sexuality and preferences. I: I is used for intersexuals; these are individuals with genitals and chromosomes who don't belong to any particular male or female binary.

A: A refers to asexuals; these are people with no sexual attraction at all. They do not find any other gender sexually attractive or pleasing. We have another term named "2 spirits," which is a newly introduced third-gender term found in some Native American cultures. These are the people who are specified as men or women by birth, but they often switch roles in real life. Furthermore, the sign (+) is used at the end of the LGBTQIA community to reflect on the fact that we have more sexualities that are yet to be discovered, and the community wholeheartedly welcomes all those who are yet to be found. So plus basically stands for anyone and everyone with any other sexual identity, as mentioned above.

Issue of Homosexuality in India

The history of homosexuality is rooted in the very deep of Indian society. The basic meaning of homosexuality is sexual inclination towards one's own gender. It's defined as the personality trait of being sexually attracted to same gender. For instance; a girl is attracted towards another girl. It's not at all a very new concept in India, it's been existing since ages and centuries. Old texts like Rig Veda and Kamasutra are a clear depiction of homosexual acts wherein, the sculptures depicts sexual acts between two individuals of the same gender. There has been instances of same-sex marriage in history of Islam. But later in Manusmriti, these acts were often associated with heavy sanctions. Such as, an individual who was found to be indulged in these acts was often subjected to loss of caste and heavy monetary penalties. Since 1974, homosexuality was considered to be abnormal in nature and a very unnatural practice. It was often criticised by society. In fact, there are instances of same-sex relationship in Hindu mythology such as Ramayan. However, with the arrival of Britishers in India, the entire view and perspective towards homosexuality began to change and there were law such as anti-sodomy laws, which criminalised same sex relationships. And it kind of generated a fear in the mind of individuals. They were scared of being indulged in any such act that led to sanctions. And even if anyone was into it they feared to express their feelings in public. Lack of legislative protections against discrimination is one of the biggest issues the LGBTQ population in India is experiencing at present. There is no federal law that safeguards LGBTQ people from discrimination in work, housing, or public facilities, despite the fact that numerous Indian states have passed anti-discrimination laws that cover sexual orientation and gender identity. They become more open to abuse, harassment, and violence as a result of their daily lives.

The general lack of acceptance and comprehension of LGBTQ people in Indian society is another problem. In India, the stigma around homosexuality and gender nonconformity is still pervasive, and many LGBTQ people experience rejection from their families and communities. Isolation, mental health problems, and even suicide may result from this. Furthermore, numerous religious organisations in India have openly opposed the practice of same-sex marriage or relationships. Additionally, there have been some major victories in the struggle for same-sex partnerships to be recognised legally. A big step forward for LGBTQ rights in India was made in 2020 when a lesbian couple in the state of Kerala received legal recognition for their marriage. This decision has not yet been enacted nationally, though.

The struggle for LGBTQ rights in India has seen some recent progress, but there is still a long way to go. In Indian society, prejudice and discrimination against the LGBTQ population are still pervasive, and there are few legal protections. In order to overcome these obstacles, the Indian government and civil society organisations must work together consistently to advance LGBTQ acceptance, knowledge, and legal protection. The lack of legislative protections against discrimination is one of the biggest issues the LGBTQ population in India is experiencing. There is no federal law that safeguards LGBTQ people from discrimination in work, housing, or public facilities, despite the fact that numerous Indian states have passed anti-discrimination laws that cover sexual orientation and gender identity. They become more open to abuse, harassment, and violence as a result of their daily lives.

Is Homosexuality Unnatural?

The natural feature of human sexuality known as homosexuality has also been seen in numerous non-human animal species. Some nations and individuals have continued the cultural myth that homosexuality is abnormal, frequently on the basis of moral or religious beliefs. The argument that homosexuality is unnatural or goes against the natural order of things, however, is not supported by scientific data.

It is crucial to remember that the idea of what is "natural" is nuanced and multidimensional. Something is not always strange or incorrect just because it is uncommon or rarely happens in nature. In contrast, homosexuality is not abnormal. More than 1,500 animal species have shown signs of homosexuality, proving that it occurs often in the animal kingdom. Homosexuality has also been documented throughout human history and in a variety of civilisations. A complicated trait, sexual orientation is presumably the result of a confluence of genetic, hormonal, environmental, and cultural influences. Homosexuality is a normal variant of human sexuality, not a choice or a sickness, despite the fact that its specific causes are yet unknown. In order to appreciate and enjoy the diversity of human sexuality, it is necessary to understand that there is no one "normal" or "correct" way to express one's sexuality. It is unfair to discriminate against people based on their sexual orientation.

Homosexuality and Religious Institutions

Religions and religious beliefs come in a wide variety, and each has its own teachings and interpretations of what is moral or immoral. Contrary to popular belief, not all religions consider homosexuality to be sinful or immoral. It is crucial to remember that one's relationship with religion or spirituality is not always determined by their sexual orientation. It is also important to remember that, although if some religious books may forbid homosexuality, they still contain teachings about acceptance, love, and compassion. People of various sexual orientations are welcomed and accepted in many religious communities.

It ultimately depends on the views and interpretations of a There is no innate relationship between religious beliefs or practices and homosexuality. However, homosexuality may be seen as a breach of some faith systems' moral precepts and by their adherents as well. It is possible for religious organisations and their adherents to perceive homosexuality as a threat to established gender roles and family structures, which might go against long-standing traditions and beliefs. Within these communities, this could lead to friction and conflict. It's important to remember, though, that there are also a lot of religious people and communities who support LGBTQ+ rights and who embrace homosexuality. In the end, it is up to each person and community to understand and live out their religious beliefs in a way that is consistent with their values and honours the humanity and dignity of everyone. Specific religious communities or individuals whether or not homosexuality is seen as anti-religious.

LGBTQIA and Pride Month

The main events of LGBTQ Pride Month, also known as Gay Pride, which is observed in June in the United States and other countries across the world, include vibrant, uplifting processions with docks and celebrities, joyous carnivals, shops, picnics, and parties. Pride Month honours the successes of LGBTQ people as well as the decades-long fight for equal justice under the law and for the lesbian, gay, bisexual, ambisexual, and queer community. But why is June dedicated as Pride Month? LGBTQ rights have been laboriously pursued in the US since at least 1924, when Henry Gerber established the Society of Human Rights in Chicago. Still, the occasion that sparked the LGBTQ rights movement passed in Chicago by Gerber. However, the Stonewall Inn incident in June 1969 in New York City's Greenwich Village served as the catalyst for the LGBTQ rights movement. In the atomic hours of June 28, police raided this well – liked LGBTQ youth purlieu, detaining the staff for dealing alcohol without a license, roughing up numerous of the guests and drawing the bar. An angry mob gathered outside as they observed guests of the bar being punched into police exchanges. In history, substantiations to police persecution of LGBTQ people had remained silent, but this time the followership booed the officers and hurled coins, bottles, and other objects at them, forcing them to block themselves inside the bar while they awaited for reinforcements.

The Stonewall screams (also known as the Stonewall insurrection), which took place outside the bar over the course of five days despite police mounts dispersing the crowd, served as the catalyst for the LGBTQ rights movement in the United States. In Philadelphia, activists had held demonstrations on July 4 as" Annual Reminders" that homosexuals and lesbians were denied abecedarian civil rights for the four times before to the Stonewall screams. These demurrers, still, had been tightly controlled keepers where men had to dress in business vesture, women had to wear skirts and blouses, and public expressions of affection were banned. On November 2, 1969, in Philadelphia during the Eastern Regional Conference of Homophile Organisations, held demonstrations on July 4 in front of Independence Hall as" Annual Reminders" that homosexuals and lesbians were denied abecedarian rights of citizenship. These demurrers, still, had been tightly controlled keepers where men had to dress in business vesture, women had to wear skirts and blouses, and public expressions of affection were banned. On November 2, 1969, in Philadelphia, the Eastern Regional Conference of Homophile Organisations, the notion of a march in kick of the Stonewall events was put out. The procession was dubbed the Christopher Street Liberation Day march after the road that served as the mecca of New York City's LGBTQ community and the position where the procession would take place on June 28, 1970, the first anniversary of the Stonewall screams.

Government's View on LGBTQIA

Numerous nations have enacted legislation recognising same-sex unions, outlawing discrimination based on sexual orientation and gender identity, and granting Transgender people legal protection. Governments have a significant impact on how society views the LGBTQIA community, and their stance on LGBTQIA rights has a significant impact on public opinion. While some governments have deliberately sought to suppress or marginalise the LGBTQIA community, others have taken steps to encourage acceptance and support for it. Overall, a wide range of factors, such as cultural and religious beliefs, political ideologies, and public opinion, affect the government's perspective on LGBTQIA rights. But regardless of a person's sexual orientation or gender identity, governments must safeguard their access to human rights.

Summary of Navtej Singh Johar Vs Union of India (Case Law)

The Supreme Court of India decriminalised homosexuality by ruling Section 377 of the Indian Penal Code to be unconstitutional in the landmark case of Navtej Singh Johar v. Union of India.

Section 377 of the Indian Penal Code, which criminalised sexual acts "against the order of nature," including gay acts, was challenged in a petition filed in 2009 by a collection of people and organisations that represented the LGBT community in India. A five-judge Supreme Court eventually heard the case in July 2018 after years of legal disputes. According to the petitioners, Section 377 infringed on the fundamental rights of LGBT people. The Supreme Court's ruling that Section 377 was unconstitutional and should be repealed decriminalised same-sex relationships between consenting adults. The court ruled that sexual orientation is a crucial element of privacy and personal liberty and that discrimination based on sexual orientation is a violation of fundamental rights.

The Navtej Singh Johar case, in its entirety, was a crucial turning point in India's legal and social history and represented a substantial advance in the country's initiatives to encourage greater openness, tolerance, and respect for variety.

Rights for LGBTQIA Community

Right to legal recognition of gender identity: Transgender people have the right to have their gender identity legally recognised and reflected on identification documents such birth certificates, driver's licenses, and passports. Right to healthcare: Transgender individuals have the right to gender-congruent healthcare treatments, such as hormone therapy, gender-affirming surgery, and mental health care. Right to education: Transgender kids have a right to an environment at school that is safe, encouraging, and free from harassment and discrimination.

Right to employment: Transgender people have the right to a job in which they are not subjected to gender discrimination identification, as well as to be shielded from reprisal and discrimination at work. Right to housing: People who identify as Transgender have the right to live in safe, affordable housing that is not discriminated against because of that identity. Right to safety: Transgender individuals have the legal right to be shielded from abuse, hasing, and prejudice in all facets of life.

It is significant to note that Transgender people's rights range from nation to nation, and even within nations, there may be various laws and policies that have an impact on such rights. Advocating for the defense and affirmation of Transgender people's rights is essential, as is working to make society more welcoming and inclusive of everyone. The lower house of the Indian Parliament, the Lok Sabha, enacted the Transgender Persons (Protection of Rights) Bill, 2019, in August 2019.

The legislation aims to safeguard the rights of Transgender people and outlaws discrimination against them in a variety of settings, such as employment, healthcare, housing, and education. Additionally, it calls for the creation of the National Council for Transgender Persons, which will advocate for the rights of Transgender people and advise the federal government on welfare-related policies and initiatives.

Conclusion

There is no shadow of a doubt that the future of the LGBT rights movement in India would be shaped by all the judgments pertaining to LGBT People. The importance of the NALSA decision and the Navtej Singh Johar decision extends beyond the acknowledgment of third-gender homosexuality decriminalisation and gender identity. These decisions, however, are also progressive because they have laid the foundation for a number of other civil rights that were previously not available to the LGBT community but are typically enjoyed by heterosexual people and cisgender people, in addition to ruling on the specific issue at hand. These civic rights include freedom, the right to freedom, the right to marriage, the right to adoption, the right to surrogacy, and more. Despite this judicial triumph, there is still a serious issue with discrimination against LGBTQ people in India. Particularly in rural areas and smaller cities, community members continue to experience social shame, harassment, and violence. Access to healthcare, education, and career prospects is a problem for many LGBTQ people. The Transgender Persons (Protection of Rights) Act, which was passed in 2019 and aims to safeguard the rights of Transgender people and grant them legal recognition, is one of the latest beneficial achievements. Activists and members of the LGBTQ community have, however, criticised this bill for being ineffective and failing to address important issues. Overall, despite some notable advancements, LGBTQ rights in India still have a long way to go.

References

Gaur, Y. (2020, June 21). *Evolution of LGBT rights in India and taking the narrative forward.* iPleaders. Retrieved April 23, 2023, from https://blog.ipleaders.in/evolution-of-lgbt-rights-in-india-and-taking-the-narrative-forward-living-free-and-equal/

Gopinath, V. (2022, September 6). *Explained | How we got here: A brief history of LGBT rights and laws in India.* TheQuint. Retrieved April 23, 2023, from https://www.thequint.com/explainers/lgbt-queer-rights-india-section-377-homosexuality-history

Human Rights Watch. (n.d.). *LGBT rights.* Human Rights Watch | Defending Human Rights Worldwide. Retrieved April 23, 2023, from https://www.hrw.org/topic/lgbt-rights

Kennedy, J. A. (n.d.). *The rights of lesbian, gay, bisexual and Transgender people.* American Civil Liberties Union. Retrieved April 23, 2023, from https://www.aclu.org/other/rights-lesbian-gay-bisexual-and-Transgender-people

Krishnan, V. (2018, December 21). "How the LGBTQ rights movement in India gained momentum." *The Hindu*: Breaking News, India News, Sports News and Live Updates. Retrieved April 23, 2023, from https://www.thehindu.com/society/its-been-a-long-long-time-for-the-lgbtq-rights-movement-in-india/article24408262.ece

Leckey, R. (2014). "Must equal mean identical? same-sex couples and marriage." *International Journal of Law in Context*, *10*(1), 5-25. https://doi.org/10.1017/s1744552313000347

Legal Service India. (n.d.). *LGBT Rights In India*. Legal Service India – Law, Lawyers and Legal Resources. Retrieved April 23, 2023, from https://www.legalserviceindia.com/lawyers/lawyers_home.htm

Outlook India. (2022, June 8). *Looking Back At The History Of The Pride Movement*. Retrieved April 23, 2023, from https://www.outlookindia.com/outlooktraveller/explore/story/71849/looking-back-at-the-history-of-the-pride-movement

Sharma, R. (2021, May 3). "Rights of LGBTQ in India and the struggle for societal acceptance." *International Journal of Law Management & Humanities*. Retrieved April 23, 2023, from https://www.ijlmh.com/paper/rights-of-lgbtq-in-india-and-the-struggle-for-societal-acceptance/

TV licence refund and cancellation – TV licensing ™. (n.d.). Retrieved April 23, 2023, from https://www.tvlicensing.co.uk/check-if-you-need-one/topics/cancellations-and-refunds-top7

Wallenfeldt, J. (n.d.). *Why is pride month celebrated in June?* Encyclopedia Britannica. Retrieved April 23, 2023, from https://www.britannica.com/story/why-is-pride-month-celebrated-in-june

CHAPTER 12

Issues and Challenges Faced by Transgenders in Contemporary World

Avilasha Sarkar

Transgender refers to individuals whose gender identity or expression differs from the sex assigned to them at birth (TGEU, 2015). Gender identity is a person's sense of being male, female, or another gender, while gender expression refers to the way someone presents their gender through behavior, clothing, and other aspects of their appearance. Transgender individuals may identify as male, female, or non-binary, meaning they do not identify as exclusively male or female (Brexit, 2023). Transgender individuals may choose to Transition to their preferred gender identity through a range of medical and social interventions, such as hormone therapy, surgery, and changes in name and pronouns. It is important to note that Transgender individuals are not inherently different from cisgender individuals, who identify with the sex assigned to them at birth (Bauer, 2018). However, Transgender individuals may face significant challenges and discrimination due to their gender identity, including legal and social barriers to healthcare, employment, and other aspects of daily life. It is essential to respect and affirm the gender identities of Transgender individuals and work towards creating a more inclusive and accepting society for all (Sessoms, 2022). Transgender individuals have historically faced discrimination, stigma, and social challenges in many societies around the world. However, there has been progress in recent years towards greater acceptance and recognition of Transgender rights, including legal protections, access to healthcare, and social inclusion. It's important to respect and affirm the gender identity of Transgender individuals, and work towards creating a more inclusive and affirming society for all individuals, regardless of their gender identity.

Introduction

The term "gender identity" refers to each person's deeply held internal and unique experience of gender, which may or may not match the sex assigned at birth. Gender identity also refers to other expressions of gender, such as dress, speech, and mannerisms, as well as one's sense of one's own body and other bodily functions. The term "gender-diverse" is used to describe people whose gender identity, including how they express it, conflicts with what is seen as the gender norm in a given situation at a given time, including people who do not identify as either male or female; the more specific term "Trans" is used to describe people who identify with a different gender. Discrimination and stigma against Transgender individuals are pervasive issues that persist in the contemporary world. Transgender individuals often face prejudice, bias, and mistreatment in various aspects of their lives, including employment, education, housing, healthcare, and social interactions. This discrimination and stigma can have serious and detrimental impacts on the well-being and livelihood of Transgender individuals, leading to disparities in healthcare, limited access to opportunities, and social isolation. Addressing discrimination and stigma against Transgender individuals is crucial for promoting equality, social justice, and human rights for all individuals, regardless of their gender identity. In this article, we will delve into the different ways in which discrimination and stigma affect Transgender individuals and the consequences they face in various aspects of their lives. A variety of international and regional mechanisms guard the rights of Transgender individuals. Nevertheless, punishing national laws, policies, and practices that target Transgender persons rob them of their rights and restrict their access to justice. These include difficult processes for updating identifying documents. As a result, state actors and society as a whole commit egregious human rights crimes. Globally, the experience of Transgender individuals is one of extreme social exclusion, which increases their exposure to HIV and other diseases, including mental health issues, restricts their access to education and employment, and eliminates their chances for social and economic success. Additionally, numerous incidents of extreme violence against a group of people who do not adhere to gender norms are a result of hatred and anger towards those people.

A Winding of Rejection and Minimisation

Discrimination and Stigma

Goffman (2009) defines stigma as, "a phenomenon whereby an individual with an attribute which is deeply discredited by their society is rejected as a result of the attribute." Goffman saw stigma as a process by which the reaction of others spoils normal identity (Wikipedia, 2023). Discrimination is when someone is treated unfairly because they belong to a certain social group (USA Hello, 2022). Homophobia, or the fear of homosexuality, as well as a general dread of people whose gender identity does not conform to traditional gender norms, are the main causes of the stigma and prejudice experienced by Transgenders. Violence against Transgenders frequently shows signs of discrimination and stigma because, at least in part, they do not correspond to established gender roles. Due to perceptions that their gender has a higher social position than the victim's, those who perpetrate violence against Transgenders may feel entitled to more authority and control. Transgender individuals in particular often face significant challenges related to social stigma and discrimination. Transphobia can manifest in various ways, such as misgendering, exclusion, bullying, and physical violence. Such unfair and exclusionary conditions fuel social weakness over a long period; Trans individuals have not many chances to seek after schooling, and more prominent chances of being jobless, consequently encountering unnecessarily elevated degrees of vagrancy (Grant J, 2011). This stigma can also result in limited access to healthcare, housing, employment, and education opportunities. Transgender individuals often face significant stigma and discrimination due to societal norms and expectations related to gender. This stigma can manifest in a variety of ways, including social exclusion, harassment, bullying, violence, and denial of legal rights and opportunities. One of the main reasons for this stigma is the pervasive belief in a binary gender system, where individuals are expected to conform to either male or female gender roles, based on the sex they were assigned at birth. Transgender individuals who challenge this binary system by identifying as a gender different from the one they were assigned at birth may be seen as deviant or abnormal by some members of society. Additionally, negative stereotypes and misconceptions about Transgender people can also contribute to the stigma they face. These stereotypes include beliefs that Transgender individuals are mentally ill, sexually deviant, or inherently deceptive. It is important to recognise that this stigma is harmful and unjust, and efforts must be made to promote acceptance and equality for Transgender individuals. This can be achieved through education, advocacy, and policy changes that ensure equal rights and opportunities for all individuals, regardless of their gender identity or expression.

Healthcare Disparities

Transgender individuals often face significant healthcare disparities, which can have negative impacts on their physical and mental health. Regular harassment and discrimination raise stress levels, which, when combined with unfavorable social, political, and economic risk factors, considerably increase the likelihood that Transgender people will have negative health outcomes. The significant differences in health between Transgender and cisgender populations are a result of structural, institutional, individual, and societal barriers to care, as well as a lack of cultural competency on the part of many healthcare professionals. Health disparities are population-specific variations in the availability, effectiveness, and utilisation of medical care. Comparing lesbian, gay, bisexual, Transgender, and queer (LGBTQ) populations to heterosexual, cisgender populations reveals health disparities in the LGBT communities. Reduced access to healthcare, postponing medical treatment out of fear of discrimination, greater rates of unhealthy behaviors (like smoking and binge drinking), and worse health outcomes (like higher rates of depression) are a few examples of these health disparities. There are several health issues that fall under the following domain such as mental Health Issues; Transgender individuals are at a higher risk of developing mental health problems such as depression, anxiety, and suicidal thoughts. This can be due to the discrimination and stigma they face, as well as the difficulties they may experience in finding healthcare providers who understand their unique needs. Hormonal Therapy and Surgical Complications; many Transgender individuals undergo hormonal therapy and surgery to align their physical appearance with their gender identity. However, these procedures can have significant health risks and complications, such as blood clots, heart disease, and infections (2007). Substance Abuse; Transgender individuals may turn to substance abuse as a way to cope with the discrimination and stigmatisation they face. This can lead to a range of health problems, including liver damage, heart disease, and addiction. HIV/AIDS;

Transgender individuals are at a higher risk of contracting HIV/AIDS due to a variety of factors, including a higher prevalence of unprotected sex, limited access to healthcare, and the use of hormone injections (Stangl, et al. 2010). Discrimination and Violence; Transgender individuals are at a higher risk of experiencing violence and discrimination, which can have a range of negative health impacts, including physical injuries and mental health problems.

Employment Discrimination

Regular harassment and discrimination contribute to high rates of stress and combined with adverse social, political, and economic risk factors make Transgender individuals significantly more likely to experience poor health outcomes. Structural, institutional, and individual barriers in access to care, along with a lack of cultural competency from many health care providers, contribute to the large disparities in health between Transgender and cisgender populations. People who identify as Transgender may experience workplace discrimination, which can have a variety of detrimental effects include underemployment, harassment, and psychological anguish. Discriminatory workplace policies; these include dress restrictions that force employees to adhere to gender standards or toilet regulations that limit access based on the sex that was allocated to each individual at birth (Raj, 2016). Harassment; when Transgender personnel are subjected to insulting statements, slurs, or jokes regarding their gender identification, either verbally or physically. Unfair treatment is when Transgender employees are given different job assignments, promotions, salaries, or other benefits than other employees.

Sex Work as a mere means of Livelihood

People who identify as Transgender are those whose gender identification does not match the sex they were assigned at birth. From their biological sex, it is different. The term "Transgender" is a catch-all phrase that refers to persons who identify as people of different genders, including drag queens, masculine women, feminine men, and others. They are classified as Transgender if they fall into the male, female, gender queen, nonbinary, or agender categories.

There is no denying that the state of Transgender people in society is depressing. However, they have always been a part of society as evidenced by the use of terms like napunsak (a person who lacks the capacity for procreation) and Tritiya Prakriti (meaning the third gender) in Vedic and Puranic literature. The way of life for the Transgender community is very similar to a depressing situation. The Transgender community has observed that the outcome has been very similar to what was predicted before observation and has been strongly connected with the condition that has already existed. Many Trans people from many locations have gathered to share one refuge, which can take the form of anything from a temple to a red light district. Guru, who is recognised as the representative of Transgender persons, is guiding them. Most of the time, Gurus are required to help people become aware of their situation. Gurus are seen as spiritual guides, escorts, and pimps. Although there are certain flaws, it has been observed that Transgender people have experienced some beneficial circumstances. While enduring hardship, they are receiving necessities like food, water, and power. It has been observed that while many of them have obtained identification cards like voter identification cards that serve as a receipt for their fundamental rights, many Trans persons who are solely dependent on sex work do not have access to such facilities. The bulk of them have never attended school, while the remainder have only completed primary and secondary education. Additionally, it has been noted that they have quotas at institutions of higher learning and healthcare. Many Trans persons who have been polled believe that until people's mentalities change and they stop seeing them as a stigma of social degradation, nothing will result in significant change. Families haven't always rejected and abandoned people who have been separated from them, and there have been many instances where families have tried their best to support their children despite failure due to society's oppressive behaviour. It also prompts gurus to relocate them to different locations where they could find work as sex workers or as beggars. However, there have been some occasions where these Transgender people have maintained touch with and visited their relatives. It has been determined from observation and interviews that the main cause of their miseries is societal oppression. They have been isolated and excluded from society, which has forced them to a distance where it is very difficult to feed them. They now feel scared and anxious, which prevents them from visiting their happy and comfortable places. There is no question that society expressly despises them and views them as "cheap human beings" who lack a sense of self. People avoid interacting with them and including them in their daily lives.

Legal Barriers

In some countries, Transgender individuals are not legally recognised, which can make it difficult for them to access healthcare, employment, education, and other essential services. The most significant problem that is faced by Transgenders is the lack of legal recognition. At the time of marriage, there aren't any well-established laws that will protect their customary marital rights, because of this their right to Article 21 is infringed as they fail to practice most things that individuals do in daily life. The right to adoption, succession and maintenance which come along with a married life are never enjoyed by them. For instance if we compare the rights that are vested on male and females with that of Transgenders we will see a huge difference. For Transgenders the rights are almost silent. For example if we talk about section 127 of code of criminal procedure which deals with maintenance and monthly allowance it won't be applicable the same way to Transgenders. In case of adoption as well there is a lack of stringent adoption laws for Transgenders and thus deprive them from the advantages of adoption. In certain nations, Trans people may not be lawfully perceived as their orientation character, which can affect their capacity to wed. For instance, on the off chance that a Trans lady isn't legitimately perceived as female, she will be unable to wed a man, contingent upon the laws of the country. Even in countries where Trans individuals have legal protections, they may face significant barriers to accessing marital rights due to societal stigma and discrimination. This can make it difficult to find a willing partner or to navigate the marriage process.

Corbett v. Corbett (AIR 1970) was the primary case to examine marriage including sex change. For this situation, that's what the Court held despite the sex change, the respondent was as yet a male what's more, a marriage between guys was void. Further, the standard utilised in the past case was applied on account of R v. Tan (AIR 1983), where, it was held that post activity of progress of sex, a male still stays a man by regulation. In India, it is seen after further thought that neither the Hindu Marriage Act nor the Exceptional Marriage Act remembers Transsexual individuals for their umbrella. Eunuchs are not safeguarded under Public Commission for Lady since they don't frame a piece of more pleasant sex. Area 2(c) of Public

Commission for Minorities which characterises minority networks as Muslims, Christians, Sikhs, Buddhists don't cover Transsexual people by the same token. Strangely, in the worldwide legitimate request, there is quiet on the situation with the Transsexual in specific records. The introduction of UDHR, the fundamental record on Common liberties, peruses "though individuals of Joined Countries have in the sanction reaffirmed their confidence in basic common freedoms" in the nobility also, worth of human individual and in the equivalent privileges of man and lady not entirely set in stone to prelude social advancement and better guidelines of life in bigger opportunity. The Sanction of Joined Countries additionally has given no spot to this gender (2005).

Conclusion

Transgender issues refer to the challenges and experiences faced by individuals whose gender identity or expression does not conform to the sex they were assigned at birth (Duchesneau, 2017). Transgender individuals often face discrimination, harassment, and violence, and may encounter barriers to accessing healthcare, employment, and other basic rights. In recent years, there has been a growing awareness and recognition of Transgender issues, with many countries introducing laws and policies aimed at promoting equality and protecting the rights of Transgender individuals (MENA Report. 2022). However, there is still much work to be done to address the systemic barriers and social stigma that continue to affect Transgender people. It is important to listen to and amplify the voices of Transgender individuals, and to work towards creating a more inclusive and accepting society (Sessoms, 2022). This can involve promoting education and awareness about Transgender issues, advocating for policy changes, and supporting organisations that provide resources and services for the Transgender community.

Transgender issues are complex and multifaceted, requiring understanding, empathy, and respect from all members of society. It is crucial to recognise that gender identity is a fundamental aspect of a person's identity and that Transgender individuals deserve the same rights, opportunities, and acceptance as anyone else. Discrimination, prejudice, and violence against Transgender people are unacceptable and must be actively addressed and eradicated. Access to gender-affirming healthcare, legal recognition of gender identity, inclusive policies in education and employment, and social support are essential for the well-being and dignity of Transgender individuals. Advocacy, education, and allyship are vital in promoting Transgender rights and creating a more inclusive and equitable society. By fostering inclusivity, understanding, and acceptance towards Transgender individuals, we can build a world where everyone can express their gender identity freely and authentically. Together, we can work towards a future where (MENA Report, 2022) Transgender individuals are treated with dignity, respect, and equality.

References

A: gender (2007a), *Gender Identity and Employment Monitoring: Best Practice Recommendations.*

Bauer, C. (2018). *Breaking the BINARY.* Pointe, 19(6), 97.

Brexit, K. (2023, April 13). *What does M F mean in text.* Speedypaper.X10.Mx - Speedy Paper. Retrieved April 23, 2023, from https://speedypaper.x10.mx/what-does-m-f-mean-in-text.html

Dls. (2022, July 31). *Regina V tan: CA 1983.* swarb.co.uk. Retrieved April 23, 2023, from https://swarb.co.uk/regina-v-tan-ca-1983/

Duchesneau, N. (2017). *Transgender rights vs "Restroom safety" in education – Green & Write – College of Education – Michigan State University.* College of Education – Michigan State University. Retrieved April 23, 2023, from https://education.msu.edu/green-and-write/2017/Transgender-rights-vs-restroom-safety-in-education/

Goffman, E. (2009). *Stigma: Notes on the management of spoiled identity.* Simon & Schuster.

Grant, J. M., Mottet, L. A., & D.Min., J. T. (2011). *Injustice at every turn: A report of the national Transgender discrimination survey.* National Center for Transgender Equality. https://Transequality.org/sites/default/files/docs/resources/NTDS_Report.pdf

Gupta, I. S. (2015). *Human rights of minority and women's: Transgender human rights.* Gyan Publishing House.

MENA Report. 2022. *Japan : The JFTC Holds the Group Training Course for Developing Countries on the Antimonopoly Act and Competition Policy,* November 28, 2022.

MENA Report. 2022. "United Kingdom : Multi-Sectoral Collaboration Contributed to Halving the Sale of Antibiotics in the UK Livestock Industry," September 30, 2022.

Raj, T. S. (2016). *Transgender inclusion: Challenges and implications.*

Sessoms, C. (2022, April 7). *How to support the lesbian community: Tips for lesbian visibility day and beyond.* Clayre Sessoms. Retrieved April 23, 2023, from https://clayresessoms.com/community-and-events/lesbian-visibility-day-2022/

Sex Matters. (2023, April 4). *Corbett V Corbett*. Retrieved April 23, 2023, from https://sex-matters.org/posts/case-law/corbett-v-corbett/

Stangl, A., Carr, D., Brady, L., Eckhaus, T., Claeson, M., & Nyblade, L. (2010). Tackling *HIV-related stigma and discrimination in South Asia*. World Bank Publications.

TGEU. (2015, April 1). *Malta adopts ground-breaking Trans and intersex law – TGEU press release – TGEU*. Retrieved April 23, 2023, from https://tgeu.org/malta-adopts-ground-breaking-Trans-intersex-law/

USAHello. (2022, September 8). *Understanding diversity in the USA*. Retrieved April 23, 2023, from https://usahello.org/life-in-usa/culture/diversity/

Wikipedia. (2023, April 14). *Social stigma*. Wikipedia, the free encyclopedia. Retrieved April 23, 2023, from https://en.wikipedia.org/wiki/Social_stigma

Wilson, E. C. (2007). *Male-to-Female Transgender Youth: Stigma, discrimination and the relationship to HIV*. ProQuest | Better research, better learning, better insights. Retrieved April 23, 2023, from https://www.proquest.com/openview/63e32bf7cd9f94f02d7cc1fffca4ee38/1?pq-origsite=gscholar&cbl=18750

CHAPTER 13

Transgender Laws and Protection of Rights in India

Rhea Eleanor Rhine

This paper analyses the psychological challenges faced by the Transgender community in India. It identifies the major issues as well as possible ways of solving these issues. The paper examines Indian legislation with regards to the Transgender community and goes into detail about the Transgender Persons (Protection of Rights) Bill, 2019 (India : Upliftment of Transgenders." 2019). Further steps that can be taken from the grassroot levels up to the highest levels of society to uplift the Transgender community and allow them to lead dignified lives are outlined and specified in this paper. This paper is based on the Conceptual Research methodology. Conceptual research is a methodology that involves monitoring and evaluating material that is already available on a certain issue. In addition, this research shows that there are innumerable challenges faced by the Transgender community and that the current legislations in our country are not enough to address all the issues that they face as well as effectively protect their rights. Various reasons, such as social stigma, traditional familial structure, bigotry and Transphobia lead to discrimination and mistreatment of Transgender individuals in the country.

Introduction

Transgender is a term used to describe individuals whose gender identity does not correspond with the sex assigned to them at birth (Katz, 2023). While Transgender individuals have existed throughout history, they have faced significant discrimination and marginalisation. However, with the growing awareness and acceptance of diverse gender identities, there is a need for society to recognise and protect the rights of Transgender individuals.

Transgender people often face discrimination, prejudice, and stigma in many aspects of their lives. This can take the form of social exclusion, harassment, and violence, as well as difficulties in accessing healthcare, employment, housing, and other basic rights and services. Many Transgender people also face challenges in terms of their legal status and recognition, as they may not be able to obtain identity documents that accurately reflect their gender identity. All of these issues can have a serious impact on the mental health and well-being of Transgender individuals (Cherry, 2021). In many parts of the world, Transgender people are also at greater risk of HIV infection and other sexually Transmitted infections, due to stigma and discrimination that may prevent them from accessing preventive services and treatment.

Historical Context of Transgender Rights

Transgender rights have been a topic of discussion for many years. Historically, Transgender individuals were not recognised or accepted within society, and they faced discrimination and violence. It is essential to understand the historical context of Transgender rights to comprehend the struggles and progress made towards Transgender rights. Transgender people, also known as *Hijra*s, have been a part of Indian society for centuries. However, their rights and acceptance have been a topic of debate and struggle for a long time.

i. *The Pre-Independence Era*: During the pre-independence era, Transgender people were recognised and respected for their unique gender identity. They were considered sacred and were invited to bless new-borns and newlyweds. However, with the arrival of British colonialism, they were criminalised under the Indian Penal Code of 1860. They were labelled as "unnatural" and "immoral."

ii. *The Post-Independence Era*: After India gained independence in 1947, *Hijra*s continued to face discrimination and marginalisation. In 1952, the Indian government passed the Immoral Traffic (Prevention) Act, which criminalised prostitution and made it illegal to live on the earnings of a sex worker. This law made it difficult for Transgender individuals to earn a living, as many of them relied on sex work as their primary source of income.

The historical context of Transgender rights in India has been a tumultuous one. From being respected members of society to being criminalised and marginalised, Transgender people have faced numerous challenges. However, with the recognition of their legal rights as a third gender, there is hope for a more inclusive and accepting society in India.

In 2014, the Supreme Court of India recognised Transgender people as a third gender and granted them legal recognition. The court directed the government to provide Transgender people with the same rights and protections as other citizens. This landmark decision was a significant step towards the recognition and acceptance of Transgender people in India.

Indian Legislation

In India, Transgender people have a long history of cultural and social acceptance, dating back to ancient times. However, in recent years, there have been some significant legal and policy developments that have sought to improve the rights and well-being of Transgender people in India.

In 2014, the Supreme Court of India recognised the legal rights of Transgender people and directed the government to take steps to protect their rights. As a result, the government passed the Rights of Transgender Persons Bill in 2015, which provided for measures such as the establishment of a national commission for Transgender people, and the creation of welfare schemes and programs for the Transgender community. The bill also recognised the right of Transgender people to self-identify as male, female, or third gender, and provided for the issuance of identity documents that reflect their chosen gender (The Hindu, 2014).

In 2019, the Supreme Court of India also ruled that Transgender people have the right to be treated as an "other backward class" (OBC) for the purpose of affirmative action in education and employment. This decision was seen as a major victory for Transgender rights in India, as it allows Transgender people to access the same benefits and opportunities as other disadvantaged groups in society.

The rights of the Transgender community were referred to as a "third gender" by the Supreme Court in the precedent-setting decision of National Legal Service Authority v. Union of India and Ors. (Sikri, 2014). The creation and regulation of social welfare programmes as well as other required measures for the defence of

Transgender rights were also requested of the federal and state governments.

The case of Anjali Guru Sanjana Jaan v. State of Maharashtra & Ors (South Asian Translaw Database, 2021), saw the Bombay High Court noting that the petitioner for the Village Panchayat elections identified herself as a female while she was a Transgender person and her application was denied (Nyaaya, 2022). The petitioner's claim was approved by the court after it was decided that she had the right to self-identify her gender.

The Transgender Persons (Protection of Rights) Bill, 2019

On July 19, 2019, Mr. Thaawarchand Gehlot, the Minister for Social Justice and Empowerment, introduced the Transgender Persons (Protection of Rights) Bill, 2019 in the Lok Sabha.

The Transgender Persons (Protection of Rights) Act, 2019 was enacted with the aim of providing a statutory basis for constitutional rights and prohibiting discrimination against Transgender persons. The Act prohibits discrimination in the matters of education, employment, health care, access to public goods, facilities and services. It also ensures the right of residence for Transgender persons in their household, and prohibits any kind of abuse or violence against them. The Act recognises the rights of Transgender persons to self-perceived gender identity, and provides for the issuance of a certificate of identity as a Transgender person (Mahawar, 2021). It also provides for the establishment of welfare boards at the Centre and in the states, and for the establishment of other welfare measures for Transgender persons.

The Transgender Persons (Protection of Rights) Act, 2019 has several important features, including the prohibition of discrimination against Transgender persons in matters of education, employment, and healthcare; the recognition of the right of Transgender persons to self-perceived gender identity; the provision of a certificate of identity as a Transgender person; the establishment of welfare boards at the Centre and in the states to provide healthcare, education, and other social welfare measures; and the prohibition of abuse or violence against Transgender persons.

The Bill clearly defined a Transgender person as a person whose gender identity is not the same as the one given at birth (National Education Union, 2019). This includes intersex people as well.

The Bill prohibits discrimination against the Transgender community on the following grounds:

i. educational services and establishments;
ii. unfair treatment with regards to employment opportunities;
iii. the denial and/or termination of employment;
iv. unfair treatment, denial and/or discontinuation of essential healthcare services;
v. discrimination with regards to full enjoyment or use of any good, service, facility, etc. that is extended to the general public for their use;
vi. right to movement;
vii. right to purchase, rent and/or occupy property;
viii. unfair treatment, denial and/or discontinuation in the opportunity to stand for public office or hold a position in public office;
ix. removal from, and access to a government facility that offers protection towards Transgender people.

The Bill also provides numerous rights for the Transgender community, such as:

i. Right of residence, wherein every Transgender individual is given the right to be included in their family. If the family cannot take care of them, the individual can be placed in a government establishment dedicated to the caretaking of the Transgender community;
ii. Right to education, wherein every institution that is funded by their respective Governments have the obligation to provide education and inclusive opportunities to Transgender persons with regards to sports, recreation and leisure activities without discrimination;
iii. Right to welfare schemes, wherein each Government shall create welfare programmes and schemes to promote and facilitate the livelihood of Transgender persons, including providing vocational training to them.

Another feature that the Bill has is the provision for the establishment of a National Council for Transgender Persons. The council will be chaired by the Union Minister for Social Justice and vice-chaired by the Minister of State for Social Justice and the

Secretary of Ministry of Social Justice along with the other members of the council being representatives from the ministries of Health, Home Affairs and Human Resources Development as well as members of NITI Aayog and the National Human Rights Commission (NHRC). Five persons from the Transgender community are members of the council along with five representatives from non-governmental organisations.

However, despite these legal and policy developments, Transgender people in India continue to face significant challenges and discrimination in many areas of life. They may experience difficulty in accessing healthcare, education, employment, and other basic rights and services, and may be subject to stigma, violence, and abuse.

Psychological Challenges

Despite the progress made in recent years, Transgender people in India still face significant challenges. Discrimination and violence against Transgender individuals remain widespread, and many struggle to access basic services such as healthcare, housing, and employment.

The educational process is significantly hampered for Transgender people as well, and many of them quit school as a result of harassment and discrimination. Few job opportunities are available to Transgender people, and those who do find employment often face harassment and discrimination in the workplace. All of this culminates in extremely negative effects on the mental health of Transgender individuals.

A study conducted in 2018 shows that Transgender individuals face a risk of having depression that is four times greater than other individuals. Transgender people may face a variety of psychological challenges due to the societal stigma and discrimination that they often encounter.

Some of the specific challenges that Transgender individuals may experience include:

i. *Internalised Transphobia:* This is the internalisation of the stigmatising cultural attitudes about Transgender people, which can result in emotions of self-hatred, self-doubt, and shame. Many individuals, especially teens, have internalised Transphobia due to familial expectations.

ii. *Body Dysphoria*: Body dysphoria refers to the internal and mental struggle faced by Transgender individuals when they struggle with their body image and the outward representation of their physical features, especially when it doesn't match their gender identity.

iii. *Lack of access to Healthcare*: Transgender individuals are often deprived of their right to basic healthcare due to discrimination. They are also denied hormone therapy, gender reassignment treatments and gender re-affirming treatments. Such medical procedures are essential to the well-being of the individual and by not allowing them to avail these treatments, they are negatively affected.

iv. *Social Exclusion*: Due to their identity that does not fit the cisgender heteronormative standard of society, Transgender individuals are often excluded in social settings, peer groups, workplace culture and many more. There is a deep-rooted stigma against them and they are extremely demeaned by society in more ways than one.

v. *Violence*: Transgender people are subject to various forms of bigotry and hatred, and their identity puts them at risk of being physically attacked by bigots, Transphobes and those who simply disagree with their existence.

All of these forms of exclusion and discrimination can have a serious impact on the well-being and quality of life of Transgender people.

Ways to Protect the Transgender Community

Transgender individuals face significant challenges in our society, including high rates of discrimination, harassment, and violence. As a result, it's important to explore ways in which we can protect and support Transgender people.

One of the key ways to protect Transgender individuals is to provide them with access to mental health resources. Transgender people often face significant mental health challenges as a result of discrimination, violence, and social isolation. Providing them with access to counselling and therapy can help them to cope with these challenges and improve their overall well-being.

Another important step is to address the economic inequality faced by Transgender individuals. This can involve creating job training programs and other initiatives designed to help Transgender people access job opportunities and build financial stability.

An important way to protect Transgender people is through education and awareness. This includes promoting acceptance and understanding of Transgender people, as well as providing information on the challenges they face. By increasing awareness and understanding, we can work to reduce discrimination and violence against Transgender individuals. Educating the public about Transgender issues and promoting the acceptance of Transgender people can help to reduce prejudice and stigma.

One of the most important ways to protect Transgender people is through legal protections. This includes enacting laws and policies that prohibit discrimination based on gender identity, such as employment, housing, and public accommodations. In addition, legal protections can help ensure that Transgender people have access to healthcare, including Transition-related care. Enacting and enforcing laws that prohibit discrimination on the basis of gender identity can help to ensure that Transgender people have the same rights and opportunities as everyone else.

Providing resources and support to help Transgender people succeed in the workplace, such as training for employers and co-workers, can help to reduce employment discrimination and improve economic opportunities for Transgender people. Ensuring that Transgender people are able to obtain identity documents that accurately reflect their gender identity and are recognised by the law can help to protect their rights and improve their ability to participate fully in society. Taking steps to prevent and respond to violence and abuse against Transgender people, including through the provision of support services and the prosecution of perpetrators, can help to create a safer and more inclusive society for everyone.

In conclusion, protecting Transgender people requires a multifaceted approach that includes legal protections, education and awareness, and supportive communities.

Advocacy

To ensure that the rights of Transgender individuals are fully protected, it is crucial that advocacy efforts continue. This can involve educating the public about the challenges facing Transgender individuals, pushing for legal reforms to protect their rights, and supporting organisations that are working to empower Transgender communities.

There is a need for more comprehensive anti-discrimination laws that specifically protect Transgender individuals from discrimination in all aspects of life (Bond, 2022). This includes access to healthcare, education, and employment, as well as protection from hate crimes and violence.

It is also important to prioritise the visibility and inclusion of Transgender individuals in all aspects of society. This can involve promoting awareness and understanding of Transgender issues in schools and workplaces, as well as ensuring that Transgender individuals are represented in political and media spaces.

There are various strategies for advocating for Transgender rights. Education and awareness campaigns can help to educate the public about the challenges facing Transgender individuals. These campaigns can also help to reduce the stigma and discrimination that Transgender individuals face.

Lobbying for legal protections is another essential strategy for advocating for Transgender rights. Legislative advocacy can help to change laws and policies that discriminate against Transgender individuals. Some of the legal protections that are necessary for Transgender individuals include anti-discrimination laws, access to healthcare, and legal recognition of gender identity.

Supporting Transgender-led organisations is also critical for advocating for Transgender rights. These organisations are often on the front lines of advocacy efforts and can provide essential support to Transgender individuals. Supporting these organisations can include volunteering, donating, and attending events.

Advocating for Transgender rights is essential to ensure that Transgender individuals have access to basic human rights. Transgender individuals face significant challenges, including discrimination, barriers to healthcare, and high rates of violence. Strategies for advocating for Transgender rights include education and awareness campaigns, lobbying for legal protections, and supporting Transgender-led organisations. We must all work together to ensure that Transgender individuals are treated with dignity and respect and have access to the support and resources they need to live fulfilling lives.

Conclusion

In conclusion, protecting Transgender rights is crucial for creating a more inclusive and equitable society. It is important to recognise and respect the gender identity of Transgender individuals and take steps to ensure that they are able to live free from discrimination and violence. Comprehensive anti-discrimination laws must be put in place to protect Transgender individuals from discrimination in all aspects of life. Advocacy efforts must continue to educate the public, push for legal reforms, and support Transgender communities. Continued advocacy is needed to ensure that Transgender individuals are able to fully participate in society and live free from discrimination and violence.

Finally, it is important for society to create safe spaces for Transgender people and respect their identity. The media and the entertainment industry can play a big role in educating the masses and promoting inclusivity. The government, the society, and each individual must join hands in creating a more accepting and equal world for the Transgender community.

References

Bond, C. (2022, November 17). *Does being Transgender affect life insurance?* Forbes Advisor. Retrieved April 23, 2023, from https://www.forbes.com/advisor/life-insurance/Transgender-life-insurance/

Cherry, K. (2021, March 22). *Mental health resources for Asian Americans and Pacific Islanders.* Verywell Mind. Retrieved April 23, 2023, from https://www.verywellmind.com/mental-health-resources-for-asian-pacific-islander-communities-5116843

India : Upliftment of Transgenders. (2019). MENA Report.

Katz, S. (2023, April 18). *"I live in a gray area": Being a Trans high school student without support.* The Nation. Retrieved April 23, 2023, from https://www.thenation.com/article/society/Transgender-high-school-harassment-community-support/

Mahawar, S. (2021, December 19). *Transgender persons (Protection of rights) Act, 2019 and its impact on the third gender.* iPleaders. Retrieved April 23, 2023, from https://blog.ipleaders.in/Transgender-persons-protection-rights-act-2019-impact-third-gender/

National Education Union. (2019). *Supporting Trans and gender questioning students.* Retrieved April 23, 2023, from https://neu.org.uk/advice/supporting-Trans-and-gender-questioning-students

Nyaaya. (2022, June 1). *Guide on the rights of Transgender persons in India.* Retrieved April 23, 2023, from https://nyaaya.org/resource/guide-on-the-rights-of-Transgender-persons-in-india/

Sikri, A. (2014). *Supreme Court of India National Legal Ser.Auth vs Union Of India & Ors on 15 April, 2014.* India Kanoon. Retrieved April 23, 2023, from https://indiankanoon.org/doc/193543132/

South Asian Translaw Database. (2021, August 21). *Anjali guru sanjana jaan vs. state of Maharashtra & ors.* Retrieved April 23, 2023, from https://Translaw.clpr.org.in/case-law/anjali-guru-sanjana-jaan-vs-state-of-maharashtra-ors/

Transgender Persons (Protection of Rights) Bill, 2019. Ch. II, V and VI, No. 40, Acts of Parliament, 2019 (India).

Venkatesan, J. (2021, December 4). *Supreme Court recognises Transgenders as third gender.* The Hindu: Breaking News, India News, Sports News and Live Updates. Retrieved April 23, 2023, from https://www.thehindu.com/news/national/supreme-court-recognises-Transgenders-as-third-gender/article5914572.ece

Wanta, J. W., Niforatos, J. D., Durbak, E., Viguera, A., & Altinay, M. (2019). Mental health diagnoses among Transgender patients in the clinical setting: An All-Payer electronic health record study. *Transgender Health*, *4*(1), 313-315. https://doi.org/10.1089/trgh.2019.0029

CHAPTER 14

An Anthropological Reflection on Transgender

Ajeet Kumar Jogi

Despite various legal interventions, socioeconomic problems and obstacles are widespread among the Transgender community; they are still confronting many social and economic issues and fighting for adequate justice. The mechanisms that address and identify the Transgender problem and challenges are crucial. Most commonly, problems and challenges appear through crime, sexual abuse, gender-based discrimination, health issue, etc. However, no stander mechanism based on the ground reality addresses the difficulties faced by Transgender individuals and the community at present. The anthropological approach and its particular research technique advocate for social justice regarding equality, value determination, role, and societal contribution. Social justice in terms of socioeconomic stability, life, liberty, and dignity is the primary need of each individual. The anthropological approach brings a broad understanding of the importance of each individual and community in society beyond caste, culture, religion, colour, gender, and region discrimination. This paper aims to understand such anthropological research techniques and concepts that help in problem identification and assessment of Transgender people from the ground. It also seeks to know how anthropological interpretation is reflected in the policy framing for Transgender people. The methodological account of this paper is based on secondary sources and a few field observations.

Introduction

The social fact on 'sex,' either male or female, must be deconstructed because society has diverse people, and Transgender is one of them. Now that time has changed, it is not like earlier when sex in the community means male or female only. This is the time of modernisation where the outer look of a person does not match sexual notions, and feeling vis-a-vis sexual notions and feelings does not match the external look. Malinowski (1929) wrote in his book "The Sexual Life of Savages" that only a synthesis of facts concerning sex can give a correct idea of what life means to a people. So, sex should be considered neither male nor female from a synthesis approach. The societal position of Transgender people regarding sex is a synthesis of male and female. Though, regarding contribution to demography and state political activities, Transgender has also had a similar position in society. However, the major problem is acceptance and valuation by the so-called males and females. Transgenderism is an individual expression than an institutional one. It should not be generalised society-based (Malinowski, 929: xx).

Now, the form of society is not based on the patriarchal and matrilineal society. There may be a mixed type of society or neither patriarchal nor matriarchal. Malinowski found that among the Trobrianders, there was a complicated attitude toward the facts of maternity and paternity. (Malinowski, 1929: xxi). Transgender has significant importance in society as an entity of family and kinship of any society that can play an essential role in society. The family itself ramifies into the clan, into the relations between matrilineal and patriarchal kindred, and all these subjects, so intimately bound up with one another, constitute one big system of kinship, a system which controls the social relations of the tribesmen which each other's, dominates their economic, pervades their magic and mythology, and enters into their religion and even into their artistic productions. (ibid). According to Malinowski (1927), the nature of the family is changeable from the previous to the present. The fact is that the family is not the same in all human societies. Its constitution varies significantly with the development level and the character of the civilisation of the people. It is not the same in the family that has changed enormously during the development of humanity.

The constructions of the third sex dominant are passed through ancient, medieval, colonial, and contemporary anthropological literature. Conceptually if we see, Transgender or LGBT people are people whose gender identity differs from the gender they were assigned at birth. Rastin (2016) says about a Transgender person, "A person whose gender does not match the gender they were assigned at birth, but is an intersex and genderqueer person." Transgender could born male or female anatomy but feel separate from their body structure because their gender expression, identity, or behaviour differs from their birth gender, hence, they try to express their gender identity in various ways. Because some people use their behaviour, dress, or mannerisms to live as the gender they feel is right for them because they reject the traditional understanding of gender, which is only between males and females. It is divided, so they identify themselves as Transgender or genderqueer. (Gupta, 2022).

Transgender person face several ignorant and discrimination. Sexuality or gender identity often makes Transgender victims of stigmatisation and exclusion by society. Similarly, ostracisation by society and sometimes even their own families view them as burdens, and excluding them is also a major form of discrimination. Discrimination is the main problem faced by the Transgender community in employment, educational facilities, housing, and medical facilities. They remain one of the most marginalised groups. Further, major problems such as poverty, land of educational opportunity, and several health issues such as mental health (Depression, stress), suicidal tendencies, HIV, AIDS, etc. According to a recent UNAIDS report in 2021, the HIV prevalence among Transgenders in India was 3.8 percent in 2021. When seeking medical care, Transgender people are frequently subjected to prejudice, ranging from rudeness and harassment to violence and outright refusal of care. Unemployment, civil status, and gender-based violence: Sexual abuse, rape, and exploitation are all serious issues for Transgender people.

These are the most common problems that Transgender people are facing even now. There is no stigma-free environment for them.

However, in light of the abovementioned issues, legal interventions have been done by the Hon'ble Supreme Court and by various civil society organisations. Several debates and discussions on various aspects of Transgender have been done at intellectual platforms like conferences and seminars. Consequentially, such legislation has been enacted for Transgender which prevents gender base discrimination and ensures the rights and welfare of Transgenders.

Legal Intervention

To protect Transgender rights and to solve existing problems, the Indian constitution has provided them with certain rights, and the Supreme Court has empowered them to recognise them as the "third gender" and also provided them with certain welfare measures. The safeguards and rights of Transgender people have been ensured through various legal instruments and landmark court judgments.

In the landmark judgment of the Supreme Court of India, in the case of National Legal Services Authority v. Union of India & Ors [Writ Petition (Civil) No. 400 of 2012 (NALSA)], Justice K.S. Radhakrishnan and A.K. Sikri in his leading judgment recognised. The Court recognised the right to self-determination of one's gender identity as male, female, or Transgender, even without medical reassignment. Further, the Court provides equal rights and protection to Transgenders under certain Articles. Transgender cannot be prejudiced on the basis of sex if it happens then it is a violation of Articles 14 and 15 because it is about the equality. Furthermore, Article 16 and Article 21. Similarly, article 19 (1) (a) on 'gender expression' and Article 19(2) on 'choice of clothing' have been insured (Gupta, 2022).

In continuation of the same, the Transgender Persons (Protection of Rights) Act, 2019, was enacted, which was a landmark law that ensures the socio-economical, educational, and health rights of Transgender people. This law prohibited discrimination based on caste, culture, religion, gender, region, etc. It also stipulates educational rights that institutions funded or recognised by the Government shall provide education, recreational facilities, and sports for a Transgender person without discrimination. About employment, it states that no government or even private entities can discriminate against a Transgender person in matters of employment, including recruitment and promotion, and every establishment) shall designate a person as the Grievance Officer, who shall deal with complaints concerning the Act. About health, it states that the Government shall take appropriate steps to provide healthcare facilities to Transgender persons, and this shall include separate HIV surveillance centres and sex reassignment surgery, and comprehensive medical treatment for Transgender persons. Insurance should also be provided.

Similarly, in terms of welfare provisions, it has provided that the concerned Government should take measures and ensure the full participation of the Transgender person in society and formulate specific welfare schemes and measures to protect the right of a Transgender person. Therefore, the Court emphasised the importance of the right to dignity and due recognition of their gender identity based on the sex reassigned after undergoing sex reassignment surgery, as a person to be recognised as male or female. Has a constitutional right to do so? Thus, Transgenders are entitled to legal protection in all spheres of state activity, including education and employment (Transgender Persons (Protection of Rights) Act, 2019).

However Transgender people are benefiting through such laws, but problems and challenges faced by society cannot be reached to the problem. The socioeconomic issue remained the same. In addition, discrimination toward Transgender is still being practiced in society. Reddy (2005) argues that representations of *Hijras* as the personification of a third sex while also challenging the sufficiency of sexual politics and gender performativity as adequate glosses on *Hijra* identification and practice. The legal rights stipulated in the laws are not being implemented. Despite the legal intervention, Transgender people cannot gain a satisfactory position in society. Even today, due to stigmatisation, they face different kinds of problems and challenges such as discrimination, humiliation, poverty, educational problem, ignorance of health care, unemployment, access to public space and shelter, etc.

Consequently, the recognition and value assessments of Transgender people and respect for their dignity and notion in society are crucial. The social recognition and value assessment of each individual in society have been done in Anthropology through several research techniques. The anthropological approach and research methods have been discussed to justify the argument.

The Anthropological Approach in the Transgender Study

The rule of law is supreme where all are same according to the Indian law and constitution. Nevertheless, the Transgender community is in a constant battle as they have to fight harassment, abuse, and discrimination from every part of society, be it their own family and friends or the society at large. Life of Transgenders are a daily battle as they are not accepted many where, and they are ostracised and ridiculed by society. That is why an anthropological understanding of Transgender problems and challenges is needed.

However, any policy or law can provide legal rights to the Transgender community, but it will remain incomplete in the absence of social recognition. Along with the governments, society also has to understand that the large population of the 'Third Gender' can contribute to the development of the country with their positivity and creativity in the same way as we are doing, just to see them as equal citizens. Need to go Because the problem of the Transgender community is more social than constitutional (Prashant Pratyush, 2018). An in-depth study is required to know the ground reality about Transgender people.

An anthropological study brings social facts into the public domain through its empirical data. Various scholars and academicians to know the ground reality through its participatory observation method have done many studies. In participatory field observation, the researcher has to live with the community, group, and individuals under the study. To know the emic perspective researcher has to stay among the community. For anthropologists to fully comprehend a culture and to refrain from perceiving other people through their own cultural assumptions, emic viewpoints are crucial.

The four-field Approach of Anthropology, Anthropology UCDavis (2023) defines,

> "Anthropology is the systematic study of humanity, with the goal of understanding our evolutionary origins, our distinctiveness as a species, and the great diversity in our forms of social existence across the world and through time. The focus of Anthropology is on understanding both our shared humanity and diversity and engaging with diverse ways of being in the world".

The four-field of anthropology are 1. Cultural Anthropology (also known as Social Anthropology). 2. Physical Anthropology (also known as Biological Anthropology). 3. Archaeology, and 4. Anthropological Linguistics. Though all the fields of anthropology are related to human being and their scientific study, the most relevant sub-discipline for the present paper are physical and social-cultural anthropology.

Indiana University Bloomington (2023) the Department of Anthropology defines, under physical anthropology, we study "Sociology and the biology of human groups. Biological anthropologists are interested in human evolution, from our origins and diversity in the past to our probable future as inhabitants of this planet. Human biology and other aspects of the discipline are studied in the context of human culture and behavior, with research in subfields such as paleoanthropology, human biology, primatology, and evolutionary psychology". In addition, in contrast, social-cultural anthropology explores the variety of human societies throughout time and geography while seeking for their shared characteristics. It employs a holistic approach, bridging the local and the global, the historical and the current, to provide a variety of perspectives on today's concerns.

It is essential to know how these anthropological sub-disciplines are related to Transgender studies. This area of anthropology works to lessen gender and cultural prejudices in research outcomes, anthropological recruiting procedures, and the creation of academic scholarship. As feminist Anthropology like Ruth Benedict, Margaret Mead and others have done. Under medical anthropology, we understand the medical composition of the body. The presence of sex hormones like estrogens, progesterone, and testosterone. In the human being, the "male" hormone, testosterone, and the "female" hormones, estrogen and progesterone, are present. However, their production sites, their blood concentrations, and their interactions with different organs, systems, and apparatus are different. Although Transgender may be different by outer look, based on hormonal presence, the sexual notion can be identified. It also put forward well-developed thoughts on ethical questions in anthropology that have generally long worked on health-related issues (Sylvie Steinberg & Laurence Hérault, 2013). Therefore, Transgender can easily identify through the lens of physical anthropology, which can play a significant role in avoiding social conflict. Under social and cultural anthropology, we study the social aspects of the Trans issue.

The advocacy of anthropology can be clearly understood through a conceptual and theoretical account. Here, theoretical and conceptual accounts like "Cultural Relativism," "Emic and Etic," and "Structural Functional" are discussed to understand the importance and contribution of Transgender people in society. The purpose of the discussion is to determine how anthropological approaches to Transgender study are able to find out ground reality beyond the social stigma. The anthropological study may be a good tool for finding Transgender problems and its solution as well.

Structure and Function Perspective

It is already written in the Indian Constitution that there should be a structure of such a society in India where there is no discrimination on the ground of caste, religion, color, sex, gender, region, or place of birth (Article 14 of the Indian Constitution). Anthropology also advocates for an egalitarian society. The 'Structural and Functional' approach of anthropology advocates for the equal importance of each member of society. According to A. R. Radcliffe-Brown (1952), "All cultural traits are functionally interrelated and form an integrated social whole. Social structure is some sort of ordered arrangement of parts or components. For instance, arrangement of persons in an institutionally controlled or defined relationship, such as the relationship of king and subject, or that of husband and wife (Radcliff-Brown, 1952, p. 11)". Similarly, social organisation is a system of roles where persons have their own roles and situation. Therefore, if we ignore the status and role of a Transgender in social structure, our social structure may collapse, and society will not be able to function. For instance, on many occasions of Hindu rituals and practices, Transgender people are invited to do such rituals, which is considered an auspicious movement by Hindu society. So, recognition of Transgender in society will be a positive initiative for the socioeconomic development of the respective society, state, and nation.

The value of Transgender in society can be understood clearly through the concept of 'Status and Role' given by sociologist Ralph Linton (1936) and Anthropologist R. K. Merton (1968). For Linton, status meant a position in a social system involving designated rights and obligations, whereas, by role, he meant behavior oriented to others' patterned expectations. Linton states the long-recognised and basic fact that each person in society inevitably occupies multiple statuses, and each of these statuses has an associated role. Each Transgender people have their own status and role in their respective society. Society is a whole set of individuals from different social institutions like family, marriage, kinship system, etc. All the social entities are correlated to each other. The status of Transgender in society can be further understood by 'ascribed and achieved 'status. The ascribed status individuals gain by birth, where achieved status gained by individual's activities in society. Transgender peoples are bisexual by birth, neither male nor female, but based on their sexual feeling, they confine themselves as male or female. Each individual has a specific contribution toward social function. Transgender people, in their respective societies, contribute a significant role. For instance, in political activities like election state cannot ignore Transgender people because they play crucial roles during the election. Another example can see in the population study. Based on the population, Government allots welfare budget for respective communities. Even without a census, it is difficult to frame such a policy. Thus, Transgender has vital status and roles as well that are essential to the function of society.

Cultural Relativism Perspective

Cultural relativity is an undeniable fact; moral rules and social institutions evidence an astonishing cultural and historical variability (Donnelly, 1984). Each society has its own culture, and member of the society has to behave according to their culture, whether it is wrong or right, bad or good, inferior or superior. The social behavior of Transgender people is a reflection of their culture. The silent feature of social-cultural anthropology is to establish equality based on cultural similarity and dissimilarity. Anthropology advocates for equality in terms of cultural value. All cultures are equal in terms of norms and values. No culture is good or bad.

Here we have tried to understand the term equality through another anthropological concept called 'Cultural Relativism. 'This concept was given by the Anthropologist Franz Boas (1887). According to Boas, cultural relativism is the view that a person's beliefs and practises should be understood in light of that person's own culture. Cultural relativists also claim that the norms and values of one culture should not be judged by the norms and values of another. On the other hand, "Cultural relativists" contend that cultural variances should be considered when interpreting human rights. According to cultural relativism, local culture rather than international ideology defines what is morally right or wrong. According to cultural relativists, human rights were created in Western nations and are founded on Western morality. Cultural relativism says that there is no value judgment of any culture.

The idea of cultural relativism holds that all moral and ethical systems, regardless of how they differ from one culture to another, are equally acceptable and that no one system is inherently "better" than any other. This is predicated on the notion that there is no absolute standard of good or evil and that all determinations of what is morally right and wrong are products of society. For the Transgender, the local moral economy of *Izzat*, or respect, is a value that provides the primary impetus for the construction of their identities (Reddy, 2005). As a result, any moral or ethical viewpoint is influenced by the cultural background of the individual. Finally, no moral or ethical system can be regarded "best" or "worst," and no individual moral or ethical attitude can be deemed "right" or "wrong."

Gurbanli (2018) cites what Fernando R. Teson (1885) writes, "The debate about the viability of international human rights, cultural relativism may be defined as the position according to which local cultural traditions (including religious, political, and legal practices) properly determine the existence and scope of civil and political rights enjoyed by individuals in a given society). Value assessments through the anthropological lens can be a good path to understanding the Transgender problem. The imperial account of T.G. in anthropology gives us a broad understanding of the Transgender problems on the ground. Therefore, anthropology advocates for equality in terms of culture, lifestyle, language, and gender expression.

Emic and Etic Perspective

To uncover emic ideas, ethnographers engage with individuals, observe what they do, and participate in their daily activities. Emic perspectives are essential for anthropologists to properly understand a culture and to avoid viewing other people through the lens of their own cultural presumptions. Social analysis with the emic perspective of Transgender is required (Don Conway Long, 1995). Etic views are explanations for behaviour provided by an outside observer in relevant ways to the observer. When anthropologists go on fieldwork, they collect data. Ethnography – the in-depth study of everyday practises and people's lives – is an important tool for acquiring anthropological data.

A "thick description," a word established by anthropological Clifford Geertz in his 1973 book The Interpretation of Cultures to describe this kind of research and writing, is what ethnography produces: a thorough depiction of the studied group at a certain time and place. The behaviour or cultural event in question is explained in great detail, together with its context and any anthropological interpretations. These explanations aid readers in comprehending the inner reasoning behind cultural norms and the significance behind the norms. This is significant since the core of anthropology lies in comprehending the attitudes, viewpoints, and motivations of cultural insiders.

The study of Transgender through an Emic perspective can give a broad understanding of Transgender life. Ethnographic field study with participatory observation among Transgender people can give an in-depth picture of the Transgender because ethnographer observes such facts while taking part in the community's social, economic, and cultural activities. Etic perspective is from the perspective of the observer.

Since there is a social stigma about Transgender that is not interacting with them, often not talking with them, and not going into their society, it is the participatory observation method of anthropology that insist we stay with them, interact with them, and participate in such activities. By participating in activities, we come to know about their life's reality. After continuous interaction with the Transgender taking part in their daily activities, understanding their cultural practices and the reason behind this would be easy. Once common people change their mindset toward Transgender, there will be no gender-based discrimination.

The ethnographical study is a research method in anthropology that has been carried out by most researchers in anthropology. Generally, due to gender bias, most people don't want to talk with Transgender people. They don't want to meet with them. They don't like to visit their place, and they don't want to know the daily lifestyle of Transgender. They don't want to know the problems and challenges that they are facing in their daily life. Even people are not interested to know their Transgender culture. Likewise, peoples are not interested to know any aspects of Transgender. In the absence of close contact and an emic view of the Transgender, many misconceptions exist in society. Whatever they hear from others is true for them. But if we interact with Transgender, we may know the different aspects of their life that we never heard about earlier. Because of the same reason, and to know the fact and figures of respective communities and individuals, the ethnographical study is very relevant. The ethnographical study insists we live among the community under the study while collecting the relevant data. The participatory approach of anthropology helps us to know the emic perspective of the problem. In the participatory field observation, we, the researcher, have to take part in any kind of social, religious, and economic practices that have been done by the community. Anthropologists have researched gender identity and expression within communities, as well as the evolution of Transgender culture as a global culture.

Transgender studies examine the experiences, identities, and practices of gender minorities and overlap with anthropology. So, in such a situation, we can't know the existing problem among Transgender. Participant observation (Malinowski, 1992) is one of the key research methods in anthropology. Sociocultural anthropologists and other academics often use it in an attempt to thoroughly understand the various aspects of a culture. Without participatory observation, we can understand the Transgender culture. What is their actual life, what is their culture, and what activities are they doing for what reasons? What is their notion? Why are they doing such practices like bagging in the train or street? Whether they are doing it knowingly or unknowingly, what are the problems facing behind that. All these short questions may be justified after close contact with Transgender people, which is possible through participatory observation.

Conclusion

Since the beginning, Anthropologist is playing a significant role in individual evaluation in society; Transgender study through an anthropological approach can be a good path to recognition of Transgender people in society without any social stigma. Therefore, Transgender is also an important entity of social structure, and they have played a significant role in their respective society. An ethnographical study with a participatory observation regarding Transgender problem assessment is needed. No individuals or groups are inferior or superior with respect to their culture and social practices. Anthropology always advocates for equality based on social norms and culture. The in-depth study on Transgender helps us in police framing and the creation of an egalitarian society. The anthropological studies prevent the social exclusion of Transgender people; instead, they advocate for equality and social acceptance. It also asserts Transgender rights and values either in society or in legislation.

References

Anthropology UCDavis. (2023). *What is anthropology? – Anthropology*. Discover Anthropology – Anthropology. Retrieved April 24, 2023, from https://anthropology.ucdavis.edu/undergraduate/what-is-anthropology

Conway-Long, D. (1995). (Trans) Gendering History and Anthropology [Review of *Third Sex, Third Gender: Beyond Sexual Dimorphism in Culture and History.*, by G. Herdt]. *Current Anthropology*, *36*(4), 709–711.

Darlong, J. L. (2023). *Status and Role*. Sociology Lens. Retrieved April 26, 2023, from https://www.sociologylens.in/2021/06/status-and-role.html#:~:text=Since%20the%20influential%20writing%20of,oriented%20to%20others'%20patterned%20expectations.)en/keywords/india

Edelman, N., & Rochefort, F. 37| 2013 When Medicine Meets Gender.

Eisenstadt, S. N. (1990). *Functional Analysis in Anthropology and Sociology: An Interpretative Essay. Truman Research Institute, the Hebrew University, Jerusalem: Israel.*

Fernando, R. (2017). "International Human Rights and Cultural Relativism." In *International Law of Human Rights* (pp. 73-102). Routledge.

Gupta, S. (2022, January 22). *What are the Rights of Transgender in India?* iPleaders. Retrieved April 24, 2023, from https://hindi.ipleaders.in/what-are-the-powers-of-the-Transgender-in-india/

Gurbanli, Z. (2018, August 12). *The universalism of human rights or cultural relativism?* Baku Research Institute. Retrieved April 24, 2023, from https://bakuresearchinstitute.org/en/the-universalism-of-human-rights-or-cultural-relativism/

Herdt, G. (Ed.). (2020). *Third sex, third gender: Beyond sexual dimorphism in culture and history*. Princeton University Press.

Humphrey, W. (2014). *The Role of Participant Observation in Anthropology*. ProQuest LLC: p. 789 East Eisenhower Parkway.

Indiana University Bloomington. (2023). *Bioanthropology*. Department of Anthropology. Retrieved April 24, 2023, from https://anthropology.indiana.edu/about/four-fields-of-study/bioanthrolopology.html

Jack, D. (1984). "Cultural Relativism and Universal Human Rights." *Human Rights Quarterly*. Vol 6 (4), 400–419.

Malinowski, B. (1927). *Sex and Repression in Savage Society*. Routledge & Kegan Paul: Landon and Henley New York

Malinowski, B. (1922). *Argonauts of the Western Pacific: An Account of Native Enterprise and Adventure in the Archipelagoes of Melanesian New Guinea*. Routledge & Kegan Paul Ltd.: London.

Malinowski, B. (1929). *The Sexual Life of Savages, in North-Western Melanesia: An Ethnographic Account of Courtship, Marriage, and Family Life Among the Natives of the Trobriand Islands*, British New Guinea. Routledge & Kegan

Pollis & P. Schwab. (1982). *Third World Perspectives on Human Rights*, in Toward a Human Rights Framework 1, 23.

Prashant, P. (2018, June 22). *Social and legal discrimination with Transgender community.* Youth Ki Awaaz. Retrieved April 24, 2023, from https://www.youthkiawaaz.com/2018/06/Transgenders-face-societal-discrimination-more-than-legal-discrimination/

Radcliffe-Brown, A. R. (1952). *Structure and function in primitive society: essays and addresses by AR Radcliffe-Brown.*

Rastin, M. (2016). "The silenced voice: Exploring Transgender issues within western choirs." *The Canadian Music Educator, 57*(4), 28.

Reddy, G. (2005). With Respect to Sex: Negotiation *Hijra* Identity in South India. The University of Chicago Press Ltd: London.

Said, A. A., & Nasser, J. (1980). "The use and abuse of democracy in Islam." *International Human Rights: Contemporary Issues*, 76-7.

Steinberg, S. (2013). "L'anthropologue, les médecins et l'expérience Transgenre." *Clio. Femmes, Genre, Histoire*, 37, 163-176. https://doi.org/10.4000/clio.11038

Suman, A. A. (2021, March 27). *Acceptance of Transgenders in Indian society and picture of their actual status.* Youth Ki Awaaz. Retrieved April 24, 2023, from https://www.youthkiawaaz.com/2021/03/picture-of-acceptance-and-actual-status-of-Transgenders-in-indian-society-hindi-article/

Teson, F. R. (1985). 1985 *International Human Rights and Cultural Relativism.* Florida State University College of Law Scholarship Repository Scholarly Publications: Florida.

The LibreTexts libraries. (2023). *4.2: Making the Strange Familiar and the Familiar Strange.* Retrieved April 26, 2023, from https://socialsci.libretexts.org/Courses/HACC_Central_Pennsylvania's_Community_College/ANTH_205%3A_Cultures_of_the_World_-_Perspectives_on_Culture_(Scheib)/04%3A_Methods_and_Fieldwork/4.02%3A_Making_the_Strange_Familiar_and_the_Familiar_Strange

UNAIDS (2021). Retrieved April 26, 2023, from https://www.unaids.org/

University of Luknow. (2023). *Emic and Etic Perspectives.* University of Lucknow. Retrieved April 24, 2023, from https://www.lkouniv.ac.in/site/writereaddata/siteContent/202004120825283934tara_bhatt_anthro_features_of_field_work.pdf

CHAPTER 15

Transgender and Social Exclusion by Family and Society

Khushboo Sahu

For an individual's growth and development in the cognitive, physical, psychological, economic, and social domains and for their group, it is essential to get acceptance and support from society and their family. In our society, gender is appropriately based on the biological sex allocated at birth; otherwise, we can argue that Indian civilisation only has two genders, namely male and female, which are adopted as the foundation of society. The majority of society does not accept people of the third gender. Their participation in work, civic engagement, economic development, social and cultural influences, education, and health is entirely excluded. Many members continue to be the victims of discrimination and social exclusion. These communities are still not frequently involved, even though other genders in our nation enjoy full access to all rights and services. To make ends meet, they panhandled, did sex acts, and danced in groups. This chapter pays particular attention to the challenges the Third Gender Community encounters as they attempt to survive and cope with the ongoing social isolation. The creation of this work incorporated all secondary sources, including a review of publications and research papers on the third gender.

Introduction

This social category was accounted for in the most recent census in India. The statistics about this community's size are mainly untrustworthy, and there is a severe lack of understanding, awareness, and information about it. Transgender individuals occupy ample space and are an integral part of our public spheres, despite their seeming absence from official records. It is common knowledge that they are asked in metropolitan areas to do their customarily allocated jobs during auspicious events. The public's response to Transgender people goes beyond their invisibilisation and includes withdrawal, disgust, wrath, and violent actions from various actors. The most extreme examples of these unfavourable and discriminatory reactions occur when group members want to use public services or facilities or communicate with authorities. This investigation focuses on the *Hijra*s in India, a Transgender population. The emphasis is on the several phases of the Transgender person's life that contribute to forming their identity as a "*Hijra*." The study also aims to understand the many forms of social exclusion that Transgender people encounter and how those reactions affect their identity. *Hijra*s are one of the most marginalised and vulnerable groups in Asian-Pacific countries, with unique issues compared to other sexual identity communities. A clear perspective of homosexuality, according to some Asian leaders, is an inappropriate imposition of Western standards that goes against Asian principles. Several Asian and Pacific Island cultures consider sexuality more fluid than Western cultures. The *Hijra* community is persecuted from economic, political, and social life. Everyone has the legal right to use society's commodities and services. Once more, society must try to accommodate this group's demands to fulfill its commitments. It is necessary to do a thorough investigation into the issues and difficulties the *Hijra* community is facing. *Hijra*s eventually stopped providing therapy services and began engaging in sexual actions, which is against India's ethical standards. The *Hijra* community has long been regarded as disadvantaged and uninvolved while making up a small part of the population. *Hijra*s are among a group of vulnerable people. The *Hijra* community has historically been the nation's most victimised sexual group. The study claims they have reportedly resisted social connections with people in the society's mainstream. Neither the government nor the general populace recognises their unique cultural, traditional, recreational, and matrimonial customs. Here we discussed problems faced by the Transgender Group.

Exclusion from Family and Social Group

Hijra people have been subjected to prejudice since birth because of how ambiguously the concept of gender is defined. *Hijra* became more conscious of their differences from ordinary guys as they grew older, particularly their frequent interactions with women and their feelings for men. Her sex-gender expectations and behaviours are generally considered unusual because they were not socially acceptable when *Hijra* was a child. India is tolerant of a wide variety of cultures; however, in that case, a family would not be able to accept their male child acting femininely. They were finally banished from their family due to their cross-dressing, the *Hijra*. These gender-specific beliefs created obstacles to their academic success. Their situation is brought on by the fact that they are not acknowledged as different gendered beings outside the male-female gender binary. They have a reduced chance of obtaining employment in the formal labour market and a higher likelihood of residing in informal settlements if they lack a postsecondary degree. *Hijra* may choose to emigrate from their families to stop further social marginalisation, or they may be forced to do so if their family members reject their way of life. They claim that *Hijra* individuals cannot attain fundamental freedoms like housing in a civilised society. Many social and religious traditions prevent burying the deceased and organising funerals; therefore, *Hijra*'s passing does not relieve them of their humiliation. In this particular situation, civil society is not giving the *Hijra* people enough attention. Every stage of their development disregards their fundamental rights and acceptance in society. The *Hijra* way of life is an example of gender-based social exclusion, showing how gender is currently ignored as part of complete social exclusion.

Many *Hijra*s have regularly lived in public spaces, including parks, train stations, and other structures. After abandoning the homes of their parents when they were young, many *Hijra*s have resided in slums or train stations. Their safety was less at risk in these hazardous circumstances than it was while they were living in a state of anxiety with their families. Racism, denying *Hijra*s basic needs, and other violations of sexual and human rights all contribute to gender and sexual orientation issues in their life (Khan et al., 2009). Because homosexual behaviour is stigmatised and the *Hijra* are not recognised as holders of distinct gender and sexual identities, their lives are in danger. A *Hijra* cannot maintain an acceptable standard of living or live in a secure social or political setting. Because they had nowhere else to turn, some *Hijra* committed suicide due to their limited engagement in social, political, and personal issues. *Palabar Jaiga* nay (no place to flee) is the expression used to describe this situation. As a result, *Hijra*s are subjected to various forms of oppression. One of many factors that make life difficult for *Hijra*s is social marginalisation. A thorough comprehension of "social exclusion" is necessary to comprehend how *Hijra*s are perceived. The maltreatment of women begins at home and continues throughout their lives. Some people were let go after assaults at work. Generally speaking, they showed a significant sense of inadequacy and self-doubt. As you can see above, out of desperation and hopelessness, they were involved in the fight for survival (Shuvo, 2018). Discrimination based on race, religion, ethnicity, gender, or place of birth is not acceptable in the eyes of the state.

On the other hand, the *Hijra* community experiences significant social stigma and is not allowed to participate in society's social, political, and economic life. The resources made available by a free society can be used and benefited by individuals. To carry out its duties, this group requires assistance from society. *Hijra*s cannot live respectable human lives in any stable sociopolitical system. Due to this, *Hijra*s in India and the region cannot completely benefit from the nation's conventional institutions and social systems. They are powerless to control events or create citizenship rights in their nation or the larger society. *Hijra*s have limited access to legal, educational, health, and social services. *Hijra* is denied because they are not accepted outside of Islam as persons of various genders. They would have had a more challenging time portraying themselves as morally upright, competent individuals. The *Hijra*s have suffered dramatically due to the moralistic views of the majority society on gender and sexuality that associate variety with immorality and destitution.

Economic Backwardness

As "Badhai" or "*Hijra*giri," most *Hijra* earn their living. Greetings, *Hijra*giri, Badhai, or bazaar tola allude to several deeds, including mugging individuals at junctions, railroad stations, and other public locations while demanding payment in exchange for blessings. Since *Hijra* is aware of how afraid people are of being cursed by them and how much faith they place in their magical skill, "Badhai" are a significant source of income for them. They now include the "*Hijra*giri" ceremony, which in cities entails dancing and singing for a newborn baby boy and collecting money from market vendors. They can also rely on begging on the streets, collectively or privately, to make a living. Traditional "Baccha Nachao" (recreation with a newborn infant) activities are less popular than they formerly were, which forces them to choose between begging and having sex constantly. A *Hijra* finds it challenging to find employment in India. Individuals identifying as *Hijra* endure severe social stigma and are less likely to possess the necessary skills to find employment. *Hijra* persons have difficulty finding work because they lack education and skills or are discriminated against because of gender nonconformity. No one wants to hire them since they are unemployed.

Exclusion from Cultural Participation

The current society framework does not view *Hijra*s favourably or as fellow humans. Since they are seen as a vulnerable minority, *Hijra* people face a lot of serious issues. *Hijra* cannot attend funerals, weddings, and family events. It is an issue because they are unable to practice their citizenship rights and because of how mainstream society has an impact. Those who identify as *Hijra* are severely excluded from social, cultural, educational, legal, and medical institutions because they identify as non-binary or Transgender. Specialisation, oneness, and monopolisation – the three Silver principles – apply to the *Hijra*'s way of life. Marginalisation rises with social stratification, much like "Silver's monopoly." *Hijra* serves as a prime example of how gender has been ignored in terms of social exclusion. Race and gender are two social and cultural constructs contributing to social isolation. Since the *Hijra* group does not conform to traditional gender roles for either men or women, gender norms do not apply to them. The *Hijra* is thereby profoundly marginalised, particularly in the dividing sexual and gender ideologies of mainstream culture that link diversity with suffering and disobedience.

Exclusion from Political and Legal Participation

Many organisations that keep tabs on sexual conduct are knowledgeable about and interested in politics and administration. Third-gender people ran for municipal office out of a sense of civic duty, but the public did not recognise them. Despite being persecuted and marginalised, third-gender people establish successful lives for themselves and demonstrate their potential. The governmental authority has been held by people who identify as the third gender in the past. The change to the Constitution has made the right to an education a fundamental right. Every citizen should have access to high-quality education, as in other nations, so the government should take all necessary measures to accomplish this. The Constitution guarantees everyone equal protection under the law, and federal legislation may be able to forbid harassment or discrimination against third-gender people. However, in our society, *Hijras* continue to lack legal standing. Society does not approve of their traditions, hobbies, or unions. The INDIA government permitted *Hijra* to designate themselves as "third gender" on official documents, including passports and national identity cards, in 2014 as a result of the NASLA judgement. *Hijras* may still experience difficulties enrolling because there are no alternatives for gender identity under this law. Remembering the discrimination, *Hijras* experienced is also counterproductive since it causes them to worry about their standing within the dominant group.

Previous Studies

Dr. Rajkumar (2016) presented a research paper based. It is a step toward increasing Transgender involvement in mainstream education, including higher education, professional education, and employment, by providing information on the educational status and issues faced by the Transgender population in India.

Bharat & Chakrapani (2014). People's Union for Civil Liberties–Karnataka (PUCL 2001, 2003) point out that In the context of Transgender issues in India, such human rights declarations are frequently broken. Transgender people have been subjected to human rights breaches, according to a report, and the discrimination they experience has resulted in violence in public places, police stations, and even homes. Most Transgender people have been forced to leave their households after coming out, either voluntarily or forcibly.

Purvis and Hunt 1999 titled "Transformations in the Discourses and Practices of Citizenship," Social and Legal Studies", proposed that Even though more individuals were participating in public life after World War II, there were still relations of dominance and subordination as a result of this exceptional economic expansion, citizenship discourses and practices changed. The variety of social identities of marginalised groups created conflict with the idea of citizenship as a universal concept. The following shows how this tension exists. The civic republican theory holds that while individuals might behave rationally to further their interests, the state should act to safeguard people as they exercise their rights. Additionally, it implied that people's political identities as engaged citizens and their right to participate in local affairs were more significant than their localised identities.

Judith Butler (1990) describes how taboos are reaffirmed and made natural by the bounds of the body as determined by social conventions. A person is said to be contaminated or has developed a lousy condition perceived as dangerous when this line is crossed. This kind of contamination or hazard only happens when the boundaries of the building are well established. In contrast, bodies based on their sex or sexuality are rejected, only serving to strengthen the culturally hegemonic identities. These predetermined boundaries of the body are maintained to ensure social regulation. The "other," who are marginalised and do not fit into the socially constructed gender binary, is created by this exclusion, which helps to solidify identities.

Miller (1998) titled "Technologies of Truth: Cultural Citizenship and the Popular Media" proposed that, In capitalist social structures, citizenship can confirm one's rights while also disciplining the cultural subjects. Numerous feminists criticised the idea of homogenising and disciplining citizenship due to its gender blindness. Due to the institutionalisation of heterosexuality, which forms the basis of the majority of this citizenship, sexual minorities are not legally protected from harassment or discrimination. Therefore, their access to civil, political, social, cultural, and economic rights that affect their individuality is restricted.

Methodology

The information is gathered from a variety of sources, including the internet, www.google.com, public meetings, census data, annual reports, gender profiles (State/Country), various constitutional bills, Wikipedia, as well as various books, journals, magazines, and types of theses that are relevant to this subject. Alternative sources the majority of the data for explorations was acquired through auxiliary sources. This study also obtained information from additional sources. Auxiliary sources include related books, articles, diaries, and other materials. This study has acquired information from the internet and used this tactic.

Theorisation

The lack of access to work, licenses, the right to vote (Article 326), and other rights has been observed as discrimination against the community. They are moreover treated like outcasts and untouchables. Every child has the right to live their life with complete dignity. Disadvantaged Transgender people are living on the periphery of society in our country. They are frequently the targets of harassment and discrimination because of their financial hardship, physical or mental handicap, or other hardships. They play an equally significant role in the nation's overall development as other kids do. Although they could be valuable human resources for the country's advancement, Transgender children have never been seen as the core of our culture since the colonial era. It is crucial to comprehend that the constitutional and legal protections the Transgender community favours will be sufficient to establish a suitable learning and social environment for the education, acceptance, welfare, and social inclusion of Transgender youngsters. Here some issues highlighted by the analysis are – 1. They are being mistreated in their own family. 2. Discrimination on the job. 3. Having inadequate educational facilities. 4. Lack of access to adequate medical and sanitary facilities. 5. Verbal and physical abuse. 6. Compulsory prostitution 7. Existential risk 8. Poverty 9. Stigma and retaliation 10. Inadequate healthcare 11. No valid documents of identity.

Result and Analysis

In this essay, we talk about the current state of the third gender, who are denied access to healthcare, education, social inclusion, and a better source of income. Government must develop better policies for these communities' benefit, ensuring that they are implemented on the ground and paper so that third genders can benefit and contribute to society's advancement. Our Constitution and rights are equally shared for each gender, and education plays a significant role in the growth of any community. All people, regardless of gender, have the right to equality and education. Education should therefore be a must for the third gender group in order to be mainstreamed.

Discussion

From the above analysis of the current situation of Transgender in India, there is a need to include a third-gender community in society, economic participation, cultural participation, educational rights, legal and political aspects, and access to healthcare facilities. The *Hijra* are individuals that exist outside of a culture that is bipolar in gender; they distort gender norms and are neither males nor females. A *Hijra* is significantly disadvantaged as a result of mainstream society's sanctimonious attitudes on gender and sexuality, which perceive variety as being equivalent to deviance and privation. Our research demonstrates that the majority of the injustices done to the *Hijra* are motivated by their gender-specific nature, which is corroborated by several older literary works. In India, *Hijra*s experience extreme exploitation, ignorance, hostility, and terrible treatment. The bulk of the culture seems to have avoided relationships with the *Hijra* population due to the current situation, which leaves them in utter poverty, ignorance, scorn, and disgrace. *Hijra*s are denied their right to full personhood and other essentials they require to survive and earn a living. The *Hijra* is not permitted to participate in society's political, social, cultural, or economic life the way other groups are. As a result, they encounter more discrimination in various aspects of their lives. The resources of society should be available to the people. Third-gendered people may be included and excluded at different times. The *Hijra* community requires society's assistance to carry out their obligations.

Conclusion

The Indian government considered the *Hijra* to be a third gender. They have continued to advocate for minorities who are denied access to social services. Although the government and humanitarian organisations have worked to solve some of the issues the *Hijra* population faces, they still face formidable obstacles. The *Hijra* people are significantly disadvantaged regarding social, cultural, political, and economic elements. They frequently battle a lack of access to healthcare, educational opportunities, and voting rights. More effects on this vulnerable sector of society may be seen if local governments and other groups work together on development projects that take their concerns more seriously and sensitively. To help *Hijra*s get into the workforce, the government has already launched several programmes. The Directorate of Social Services is involved in many initiatives for the *Hijra* community, including identity cards, scholarships for *Hijra* students to pursue higher education, the empowerment of *Hijra* youth through employment in income-generating activities, socioeconomic development, and social security for the elderly *Hijra* population, among others. India is the first country to introduce the social characteristics of *Hijra*s and the degree of help they receive from their relatives for their employment, health, and education. Because of the Supreme Court's decision, it is evident that the *Hijra* community is now more widely accepted within their community as a third gender. The third gender issue must be included in the national school curricula for our kids to comprehend it properly. As a result, society will respect third-gender people more and be better able to appreciate diversity. The way the *Hijra*s wish to be accepted by society must be discussed and debated before any decisions are made. Legislation acknowledging *Hijra* as a legitimate third gender must be passed to increase societal acceptance and access to government social assistance. State organisations are accountable for ensuring equality and opportunity for everyone.

References

Bay, B. (2019, November 27). *Time to change our anti-Hijra bias.* The Daily Star. Retrieved April 21, 2023, from https://www.thedailystar.net/opinion/magic-madness/news/time-change-our-anti-*Hijra*-bias-1829326

Babbar, S. K. (2016). "The socio-legal exploitation of the third gender in India." *IOSR J Humanit Soc Sci*, *21*, 12-8.

Chakrapani, V., & Bharat, S. (2014). *Getting to zero? A national survey on HIV-related stigma and discrimination in urban India.* URL: India, http://www.in.undp.org/content/dam/india/docs/HIV_and_development/HIV%20r elated%20stigma%20Low%20Res%20all%20pages%20LR.PDF

Department of Social Services. (2022, December). *Livelihood Development Program for the Hijra Community:.* Department of Social Services: Government of the People's Republic of Bangladesh. Retrieved April 21, 2023, from https://www.dss.gov.bd/site/page/e3108b96-8e64-4fb4-be8e-3f2f8e9d27bb

Khan, S. I., Hussain, M. I., Parveen, S., Bhuiyan, M. I., Gourab, G., Sarker, G. F.,. .. & Sikder, J. (2009). "Living on the extreme margin: social exclusion of the Transgender population (*Hijra*) in Bangladesh." *Journal of health, population, and nutrition*, *27*(4), 441.

Magre, B. (2012): "Understanding Education and Employment of Hijaras of Mumbai," *MA thesis, Tata Institute of Social Sciences*, Mumbai

Mal, S. (2015). "Let us to live: Social exclusion of *Hijra* community. "*Asian Journal of Research in Social Sciences and Humanities*, *5*(4), 108-117.

Marshall, T. H. (1950). *Citizenship and Social Class and Other Essays.* Cambridge: Cambridge University Press

Miller, T. (1998). *Technologies of Truth: Cultural Citizenship and the Popular Media*, Minneapolis: University of Minnesota Press.

Nanda S (1999). Neither Men Nor Women: the *Hijra*s of India. London: Wadsworth.

People's Union for Civil Liberties–Karnataka (PUCL-K), (2001): "Human Rights Violations against the Sexual Minorities in India: A PUCL-K Fact-finding

Report about Bangalore," http://www.pucl.org/Topics/Gender/2003/sexual- minorities.pdf.

People's Union for Civil Liberties – Karnataka. (2003). *Human rights violations against the Transgender community.* Retrieved April 21, 2023, from https://queeramnesty.ch/docs/HR_Vioaltion_Transgender_India_PUCL2003_text.p df

Purvis, T., & Hunt, A. (1999). *Identity versus Citizenship: Transformations in the Discourses and Practices of Citizenship. Social & Legal Studies*, 8(4), 457–482. https://doi.org/10.1177/a010358

Rajkumar, D. (2016). "Education of Transgenders in India: Status and challenges." *International Journal of Research in Economics and Social Sciences*, *6*(11), 15-24.

Sawant, N. S. (2017). "Transgender: status in India." *Annals of Indian Psychiatry*, *1*(2), 59.

CHAPTER 16

Violence and Discrimination against Transgender

Anju Harbansh

Gender-based discrimination and violence are menaces rooted in India. One of the pertinent issues is discrimination and violence against Transgender persons. A Transgender is a person whose gender identity differs from the sex of the person at birth. Their gender behaviour or identity does not match their biological sex from the time of their birth. They have been the most marginalised, forgotten and deprived sections of Indian Society and face discrimination and violence as compared to other genders. When the landmark NALSA judgment came, the Transgender Community was elated and contented. It was expected that an optimum shift would take place in the attitude of society towards the community. However, the results lack enthusiasm. The lack of implementation of that judgment is the reason that they are still fighting against discrimination and are not recognised in society. This research paper will look at the various forms of discrimination faced by the third gender. The paper would also see Transgenderism in the current scenario highlighting the changes brought on account of the judgment. The article will also look at various legislations and schemes brought by the government for the upliftment of the third gender. This article is purely based on secondary data. The data is collected from journals, newspapers, research articles, and the Internet and govt. reports. The present situation of Transgender, their rights, health and constitutional rights are discussed in this article.

> "Sex is what you are born with, gender is what you recognise and sexuality is what you discover"
>
> – Anitha Chettiar

Introduction

In Ancient India, the *Hijaras* of *Kinnars* have a recorded cultural history which relates back thousands of years. Their references can be seen in Hindu texts such as Mahabharata and Ramayana. One of the many forms of lord *Shiva* involves him merging with his wife, *Parvati*, to become *Ardhanari*, who holds significance in the community. The depiction of this community was often the theme of art and paintings like sculptures in *Sanchi*, *Ajanta*, and *Amaravati*. They held important positions in courts and various administrative duties during the Mughal era in India. In India, Transgender is known by different names like "*Hijras, Kinnar, Jogtas, Joggapas, Khusras* and *Shiv Shaktis*". Aghast feeling captives our hearts with the persistent rise in violence and discrimination faced by minorities in the second largest democratic country in the world. Gender-based violence against Transgender came to light through newspapers and media. Violence against Transgender person is often a manifestation of stigma and discrimination because they do not fit into traditional gender categories.

A person who identifies as Transgender is one whose gender identity differs from their sex at birth. From the moment of their birth, their gender conduct or identity does not correspond with their biological sex. It is interesting to note that, unlike any other social norms and rules, human behaviour towards Transgender have deteriorated. The Transgender community was euphoric after the landmark NALSA judgment came in 2014. It was expected that society would recognise them in a humanistic light. However, the results were far away from this dream. The *Hijra* community still faces low social standing. Some days they are considered auspicious, and some days cursed for their presence. The Transgender or *Hijra* community is still revered by society at large. They are often victims of hate crimes and abuse. It is believed that they do not fit into gender binary norms and stereotypes of our society. They have been ignored by our society at large except when they are rewarded during festivities. According to the 2011 census, there were around 4.88 lakh Trans-people in India. They are considered in large numbers but are not considered human beings and face exclusion from society to this date. Despite many years, the issue of Transgender is still a matter of question in societal and cultural contexts. Gender equality remains a challenging factor towards the development of society owing to the existence of gender stratification prevailing within the social structure of India. Nevertheless, few people have risen, irrespective of all bigotries and troubles and have made a name for themselves. In this paper, the researchers will discuss the discrimination issues encountered by Transgender persons. The paper would also analyse Transgenderism in contemporary times while drawing inferences from the famous NALSA judgment. We will discuss the welfare schemes and initiatives started by the government and critically scrutinise the Transgender Person (Protection of Rights) Act, 2019 in the later part.

What Does It Mean To Be A Transgender?

The term Transgender (T.G) is used in the form of an umbrella to include a wide range of identities and expressions of people contrary to their biological sex and not limiting it to Transsexual people only. There are four types of people categorised in the umbrella definition they are – (1) Persons whose gender identity or expression or behaviour does not conform to their biological sex. (2) Transgender people may also include identity to their sex assigned at birth. These persons do not identify as either male or female, commonly referred to as *'Hijras/Eunuchs'*. They are neither men by reason of anatomy or appearance and nor women as they lack a female reproductive system. They are claimed as 'third-gender' because of the absence of procreation abilities. Among *Hijras*, there are emasculated men (castrated, nirvana), non-emasculated men and intersected persons(hermaphrodites). (3) Transgender includes persons who intend to undergo sex reassignment surgery (SRS) or have undergone SRS to align their biological sex with their gender. They are called 'Transsexual persons". (4) There are persons who wear clothes designed for the opposite sex or cross-dress in contrast to their gender. They are called Transvestites. They are not usually Transgender but just feel comfortable wearing opposite-sex clothes. They prefer to be described as 'Cross-dressers' (Delvin, 2015).

Theoretical Framework

Chettiar A. (2015) examined the socio-economic status of *Hijra*s to understand the problems faced by them with special reference to their health and the harassment faced by the police. Among the *Hijra*s, about half of them belonged to the middle class, and about 40% belonged to the upper and lower class. Likewise, Divan et. al. (2016) explained that the United Nations Development Programme

(UNDP) furnished literature on the Transgender community's human rights, health issues, and socioeconomic issues and also mentioned solutions for these problems. This document addressed countries to take action immediately to tackle the infringement of human rights of Transgender persons, the prevalence of HIV, poverty and humiliation suggests encouraging social acceptance, superior health services, impartiality and socio-economic development. Similarly, Konduru & Hangsing (2018) explained the problems of Transgender's sociocultural elimination, their growth and the attitudes of society towards them. Even after Supreme Court recognised Transgender as the third gender, they still face elimination from social, cultural, political and economic fields. Society should have a positive attitude towards them and accept them for giving dignified life. Sameeta et. al. (2018) describes the connection between socio-demographic factors and subjective well-being among fifty Transgender aged 18 years and above in Manipur. The results show no significant connection between subjective well-being and socio-demographic parameters like age, educational qualification, profession, dwelling and outlook of family. Sivakami & Veena (2011) explains that thirty-five per cent of participants had felt harsh Transgender identity stigma, whereas 49 per cent of participants had felt reasonable stigma. Only 44% of participants felt a good quality of life (QOL), while 35% of participants reported very poor QOL. The QOL of participants depended on their acceptance or nonacceptance by their family members.

Violence and Discrimination against Transgenders

Transgender people face discrimination every face of their life because they do not fit into the gender roles of society. Every Transgender person must have encountered verbal, sexual and physical violence at least once in their life. Transphobia is also the biggest reason for such discrimination and violence against these people. Transphobia is a form of hatred, disbelief, terror, fear or distrust for Transgender people or people whose gender expression does not conform to traditional gender roles. This causes them to live a life of anxiety and worry. They are afraid of constantly being judged. The areas where Transgender person commonly face abuse are-

1. *Employment* – Transgender persons face extreme difficulty in finding suitable jobs and work of their choice. They are

forced into sex work, begging and dancing in bars etc., due to social discrimination in employment. Apart from low levels of literacy in the community, they become socially, politically and economically powerless in society. In most of the forms, there are only two categories of gender which are male and female, because of which many Transgender people couldn't even apply for these jobs. Here are some instances where the bright future of some persons was thrown into abysmal. In Tamil Nadu, a young athlete got selected to the police force, but her medical examination revealed she was Transgender and was dismissed from the job, although women had other qualifications. Similarly, in Maharashtra, a young woman was dismissed from her service even after qualifying because police forms did not recognise Transgender as a gender. Another young woman in Tamil Nadu was not allowed to appear in the UPSC exam because she was Transgender, and again UPSC only recognise two gender categories i.e. male or female. She filed an appeal and RTI, but she was not allowed to appear in the exam. Presently this situation has changed after the NALSA judgment recognising Transgender as the third gender.

According to a survey conducted by NHRC, 89 per cent of Transgender persons do not get employment opportunities despite having the qualifications and skills which is required for a job. Partially being the reason to be compelled to do sex work for livelihood. During the Covid-19 pandemic lockdown, these Transwomen faced more difficulty in getting employment as most of them depend on sex work or blessing/ begging as means which was impossible during the lockdown.

2. *Education* – According to the 2011 census of India, literacy amongst Transgender persons was 46 per cent compared to 74 per cent of the general population. According to research conducted on 120 Transgenders in Coimbatore city, 56 per cent of persons have primary and middle school education. Some of them hesitated to go to school after noticing the changes in them, and 64 per cent of them belonged to the low-income group. According to an NHRC report, 52 per cent of Transgender person left school because they faced harassment by classmates, and 12 per cent of Transgender

people left because they were harassed by their teachers in school. Formal education was a far-fetched dream for such people whose whole life is judged by gender identity. Fear of being discriminated against is the result that Transgenders do not have a substantive number in higher education and universities.

3. *Family* – Transgender people face discrimination and violence mostly because of societal expectations, which leads to Trans-children often being reprimanded, blamed and criticised by their family members. According to a study by the National Institute of Epidemiology, around 60,000 Transgender persons across 17 states, including Tamil Nadu, found that a large population of persons received no support from their biological parents. Parents disown and evict their child because they feel it would bring disgrace and shame to the family and often have effects on other children of the family. Also, Transgender persons find it difficult to claim their share of the property or inherit those properties that would be lawfully theirs. Sometimes teenagers or children decide to run away from their house because they are not able to tolerate the abuse and discrimination by their families. According to a study conducted by the Kerala Development Society on behalf of the National Human Right Commission, only 2 per cent of Transgender person live with their family.

4. *Exclusion from Health Services* – Transgender person's health problems do not find a place in the top agenda of the government list. Transgender people face worldwide substantial health disparities and barriers to accessing appropriate healthcare services. A Transgender person is more likely to face sexual violence and harassment as compared to the general population who contracts HIV. The risk of developing mental health issues, often resulting in suffering depression and likely to attempt suicide, increases gradually. Transgender communities experienced discriminatory treatment by healthcare providers and refusal by many healthcare insurance programmers to cover services for Trans persons. The National AIDS Control Organisation (NACO) in 2015-16 noted the rate of HIV prevalence amongst Trans-population to be 8.82%, the second highest among the high-risk groups. HIV prevalence among the

Transgender community is estimated to be 8.2 per cent. A range of social, economic and legal factors contribute to the increased risk of HIV faced by these people. The Pehchan project works with Transgender people across 18 Indian states to increase their access to health, social and legal services.

5. *House Accommodations Problems* – Transgender persons often face discrimination in accessing houses for accommodations which include discrimination in the rental market, high rents, and refusal of housing facilities; even if they get houses, they are subjected to harassment from landlords and neighbours. Housing is a serious problem for a Transgender person also lack of identity documentation is also the reason that accommodation facilities are denied to these people. In Kochi, 21 Transgender people were appointed for jobs in Metro Services, but in one week, out of 21 Transgender people, eight have quit their job and the reason being nobody is ready and willing to give houses and rooms on rent to them.
6. *Gender-based violence* – Transgender persons face violence like sexual violence, physical violence, assault etc., simply because of who they are. The numbers of violence against these people a much higher as some often go unreported. They have been facing most of the violence from their own families, friends and partners. The government collects every year NCRB data which shows the crime against a person committed, but there is no specific mention of crimes committed against Transgender persons. A female-identified Transgender person A. Revathi, in her autobiography "Truth about Me", narrated how she suffered violence in her school she explained that

> "At school, I felt fear looking at the big boys, those in Classes 11 and 12. And they were always on the lookout for me. They had marked me out from the others. Whenever I walked past them on the school grounds, they would yell, 'Hey girl-boy' and hit me on the head with their balled up fists. They would pinch me on my chest, and taunt me saying, 'When you played Chandramathi, what did you stuff your chest with?' On the days this happened, I did not want to sit next to the boys in my class, for I felt coy and shy."

On 2 December 2017, Bhavitha, a Transgender person from Telangana, was found dead near a dustbin. The police did not allow her sisters and other *Hijra* persons to claim her body because only the blood relations and parents can lay such claims.

7. A PIL filed by Karan Tripathi sought separate data on Transgender prisoners in the NCRB reports. The Central government told the Delhi high court that Transgenders will now be included as a separate gender in National Records Bureau's Prison Statistics Report 2020 onwards.
8. *Discriminatory Laws* – Indian Courts recognised Transgender persons as the "Third Gender". But we still have discriminatory laws like there is no law which supports the marriage of Transgender persons and having a spouse and setting up of their own family. Recently cabinet approved the Surrogacy (Regulation) Bill 2020, which allows surrogacy for divorcees, widows, heterosexual couples and single women as well but the bill is completely silent on the right of parenthood of Transgender people. Even the adoption laws do not allow Transgender persons to legally adopt children. Sometimes they do it illegally to support children who are run away or abandoned by their families. Gauri Sawant, a self-identifying *Hijra*, plays the real-life role of mother to her adopted daughter. Motherhood is often perceived as a gender norm which requires it to fulfil the womanhood criteria. There is an urgent need to revisit the notions of motherhood and adoption. We need to look above marriage and kinship outside the binary gender sex.

   Section 377 of the Indian Penal Code, 1860 was struck down as discriminatory in nature and decriminalised the same sex between homosexual people. Also, the new Transgender Persons (Protection of Rights) Act, 2019 is also discriminatory in nature and gives punishment between 6 months to 2 years if a sexual offence is committed against the Transgender person which is lower in comparison to crime committed against women.
9. *Societal Response* – From ancient times, our society has condemned and not acceptable to those people who do not conform to its societal norms. The Transgender community is one such group who have been discriminated against, marginalised, abused and neglected in almost every known society. They are invisible in society. They are not invited to

any functions, weddings and other social activities. According to NHRC, survey 99 per cent of Transgender persons who participated in the survey accepted that they have had social rejections more than once in the past. Families and other social organisations usually ostracise these persons and face social exclusion in every phase of their life.

10. *Lack of legal Redress* – Before the Transgender Persons (Protection of Rights) Act, 2019, there were no special dealings with the right of Transgender persons. There is various kind of abuses done with Transgender person, like sexual violence and physical violence, which violate their basic human rights and right to live with human dignity. They are raped, gang raped, arrested arbitrarily, physically assaulted and much more. Access to justice for Transgender people is at a lower level, they are not supported and helped by police if they approach police for justice. Instead faced harassment by police officers, and police demand bribes to see their case because of this, they discourage them from approaching the police. Transgender people faced the lack of basic recognition before the law, which impedes them to recourse for the crime which is committed against them.

11. *Gender identity issues* – In India, gender expressions combine only masculine and feminine elements, and this is the reason that Transgender persons encounter severe discrimination in India. Gender generally determines every aspect of the life of every individual, including name, clothes, appearance, behaviour, occupation, mobility etc. Every document which identifies the person, such as a passport, driving licence, mark sheets, Aadhar card, pan card etc., carries the gender identification also, even the public utilities like toilets in malls, airports, changing rooms, also security check airports, and other public places are gender specific in India. India is gender specific country, and the right of Transgender to have own their identity has been denied. There is a lack of understanding of the complexities of their biological sex and the gender identity of the Transgender community.

    On 15th April 2014, the apex court passed a NALSA judgement which recognised Transgender people as the 'Third gender' and thus forgoing the binary gender system of the country. The court gives the right to self-determination of gender by giving psychological test over the biological test and thereof give recognition in the law. They also placed obligations to the central and state government to create a legal and political environment which allows Transgender persons to access their rights and reach their full potential in society. Due to a lack of proper documents, many Transgender students couldn't get admission into universities.

Analysis of Transgenderism in Contemporary Society

Right to live with dignity

The apex court in National Legal Services Authority v. Union of India24 relied on the principles of Transformative constitutionalism and hold that constitution must guide the society toward a pragmatic approach where fundamental rights are fiercely guarded. Constitutional morality would prevail over societal morality to ensure that the human rights of the LGBT community are protected. The court held that gender identity is intrinsic to one's personality, and denying that would be violative of one's dignity. The court affirmed that consensual carnal intercourse between adults is it homosexual or heterosexual, in private space does not in any way harm public decency or morality. Sec 377 was violative of Art 19(1)(a). The right to choose a partner of his or her choice is a facet of individual liberty. The right to live with dignity has been recognised as a human right on the international front and by the number of precedents of this Court and, therefore, the constitutional courts must strive to protect the dignity of every individual, for without the right to dignity, every other right would be rendered meaningless. The Apex Court held that Transgender persons were entitled to fundamental rights under the Constitution of India. Art. 14, 15, 16, 19(1)(a) and 21. Further, the court referred to international treaties and Yogyakarta Principles to recognise Transgender person's human rights.

Right to have an identity

It is estimated at 75 per cent of Transgender people have not obtained Aadhar Cards. They are deprived of basic facilities like PAN cards and Ration cards to get government subsidies. In 2005, the Indian passport application forms were updated and mentioned the third gender in their form. Although it is still not a uniformly applied practice. In a Special leave petition filed by Human Network,

Reshama has challenged the September 19, 2017, order passed by the High Court at Patna dismissing her petition for self-identify as the Third Gender in PAN for the purpose of linking PAN and Aadhaar and to avail of the associated benefits. In a win for the entire Transgender community, the Centre has amended the Income Tax Rules, 1962, to allow Transgenders to be recognised as an independent category of applicants for obtaining a Permanent Account Number (PAN) for their tax-related Transactions.

Right to vote and participate in elections

Under the Constitution of India, every citizen has the constitutional right to vote and compete in elections. Till 1993, the electoral ballots had only two categories of gender i.e., male and female. In 1994 Transgender persons were allowed to participate in the voting process. Since then, the election commission recognised 'Eunuch' as a citizen. Some of them contested in general elections for seats of Members of Parliament in 2014. On 12th March 2021, BJD member Sasmit Patra introduced the Constitution (Amendment) Bill 2020 (substitution of articles 331 and 333) in the Upper House, which provides for the reservation of Transgender in parliament and state assemblies.

Right to marry and adopt children Transgender

Persons are yet to exercise their democratic rights in marriages, adoption or raising a child regardless of being recognised as Transgender. A strong contention in favour of providing adoption facilities to this community is no one from the general population would come forward to adopt a Transgender child who either maybe a runaway or be abandoned. Since time immemorial, this community has often taken care of such children now, what is wrong if they want to legally adopt such a child who is already adopted in every sense? Formerly section 377 of IPC was nothing but the manifestation of the Victorian era, where sexual activities were only for the procreation of children. The traditional concept of marriage for the procreation of children has to be updated with the evolution of the concept of sex. With the advent of technology, especially in medical sciences, procreation is possible through different means like IVF, sperm donors, and freesing eggs. Social morality changes from time to time. Five-judge bench unanimously held that Sec 377 of the Indian Penal Code, 1860, insofar as it applied to consensual sexual conduct between adults in private, was unconstitutional. However, the court has not said anything in regard to their right to marriage adoption. It is expected in future that the Apex Court would shed some light on this regard.

Mental Trauma Faced by Transgender Children

Transgender children have substantially higher rates of anxiety and depression as compared to cisgender. Children, especially teenagers, are constantly in threat of being judged for their sexual preferences in contradiction to their gender. The children are often not supported by their parent's succumbed to societal pressure. The psychological changes undergone by a child who is attracted to the same sex or like to cross-dress and change of sexual orientation are left unheard. Leading them to believe they are different from others. Social media also plays a role in changing today's modalities of society. What is considered cool and not fitting the threshold has left children exposed to myriad beliefs. Imagine the pressure on children to befit such norms and how difficult it would be for a Trans child who is trying to understand the genetic changes undergoing their bodies. Reports suggest that Transgender children who are supported in their gender identity have normative levels of depression and only minimal levels of anxiety. The study suggests that anxiety, depression, and sociality associated with Transgender children are not inherent but rather are the result of bullying, rejection and disrespect.

Shortcomings of Law

Before 2020, we did not have a law which addresses the rights of the Transgender community. To give effect to the decision by the apex court, parliament passed the Transgender Persons (Protection of Rights) Act, 2019, intended to benefit the community. However, the act was heavily criticised for failing to consider the ground realities and for not being efficient in protecting the interests of the Transgender community. Some critical points are –

i. *Protection from discrimination* – the act provides for protection against discrimination against employment and healthcare which is also guaranteed under the Constitution of India. However, no penalty has been prescribed against the person who discriminates against a Transgender. It does not talk about monetary compensation as a relief against discrimination.

ii. *Recognition of identity* – the act provides for recognition of identity. A Transgender person can make an application to District Magistrate to receive a certificate of identity. This procedure of obtaining a certificate, however, seems contrary to the spirit of judgment. The judgment states that self-determination of the ender is an integral part of personal autonomy and falls within the ambit of persona; liberty guaranteed under the Constitution of India. The act provides for the right to self-perceived identity, but it is unclear as to what this right entails.

iii. The act does not address the aspects of the procedure to obtain a certificate of identity. As

Example:-

- It does not have a procedure to be followed before the issuance of a certificate
- No appeal provision if the certificate is refused
- Procedure to rectify the defects, if any, in the certificate
- Rights of residence, surrogacy, adoption, and marriage have not been mentioned.

iv. *Reservation* – the NALSA judgment directed the government to treat the Transgender community as a "socially and educationally backward class" and give them reservations in admission to educational institutions, jobs etc, but the act is silent on this issue. v. Medical care – The community alleges that the act does not provide a definite plan with concrete steps to implement the health care services and medical facilities apart from being on paper. It does not address the plight of victims of abuse by providing counseling, hormonal therapy etc.

v. *Penalties* – The punishment given this act is discriminatory in nature. "if someone sexually abuses or harasses a Trans person, then the culprit gets a jail term up to 2 years". It means they are not looking at the victim as human but seeing them through the lens. The punishment seems to be rhetoric in nature. If a Trans person considers herself a woman, then why can't she have the same rights as that woman subjected to sexual harassment? It does not provide any information on failure to designate a compliance officer to deal with complaints in case of violation of the law. vii. The act fails to address the sexual, physical or mental assault. It doesn't, for instance, talk about gender-neutral laws and punishments like rape, murder, and hate crimes.

vi. The act nowhere mentions any rights provided to a citizen of India on account of being recognised as a gender. The issues of marriage, inheritance, parenthood, surrogacy and adoption are left unattended.

vii. The National Council for Transgender Persons made under the act does not have a procedure for regular meetings or annual reports of areas of development.

viii. The provisions do not address the issues of challenges being faced by violence from families, being outcasted etc rather require them to send to a rehabilitation centre. One is compelled to think if segregation and relocation are really answers to these issues. The act was passed without any debate in Lok Sabha on the same date when the proposal of abrogation of Art. 370 of the Constitution was introduced. The bare reading of the act shows the hastiness of providing a law for the Transgender community. The Transgender community termed the day act was brought as 'Gender Justice Murder Day'. Unless these points are addressed, the protection sought for Transgender person will be a futile exercise.

12. Initiatives taken by the government for Transgender persons

In the landmark judgment of National Legal Services Authority v. Union of India, courts criticised the government for such discrimination against these people. The court further directed the central and state governments to take steps for the advancement of the Transgender community, including recognising the third gender as a "socially and educationally backward class of citizens" entitled to reservations in educational institutions and public employment and to frame social welfare schemes for the community.

- *Tamil Nadu:* Tamil Nadu was the first state who has shown unprecedented efforts to protect Transgender people and access them to social protection schemes of the State and Central governments. They provide free sex reassignment surgery for Transwomen in selected government hospitals in the state. They have given full scholarships and free housing facilities and issued notice to schools and colleges that Transgender people will not be denied admission. Tamil Nadu government has also offered training and financial assistance of Rs.20 thousand for the welfare of this community. Tamil Nadu government, through the welfare board, has issued identity cards to Transgender people so they easily get rations and other welfare schemes. Also, the media of Tamil Nadu has played a very important role in creating awareness about the rights of Transgender people. The Tamil Nadu government has also created a database for Transgender people, which is also a very big achievement.

- *Karnataka* – Karnataka state has established several welfare boards for the protection of human rights issues of the TG community. 'Mythri' pension scheme is launched for the Transgender people under which people between the age group of 18 to 64 are entitled to receive 500 rupees monthly pension also the people with annual income less than 17,000 in urban areas also people in the rural area annually income less than 12,000 are eligible to get the benefit of this scheme.
- *Delhi* – The government of Delhi provides 1,000 rupees per month to Transgender people who are living in Delhi for 3 years. found that thirty-five per cent of participants had felt harsh Transgender identity stigma, whereas 49 per cent of participants had felt reasonable stigma. Only 44% of participants felt good quality of life (QOL), while 35% of participants reported very poor QOL. The QOL of participants depended on their acceptance or non-acceptance by their family members on 15th July 2015 West Bengal government set up a separate welfare board for the Transgender person and recognises Transgender people as third sex so they can seek to address all the grievances. For the welfare and their social recognition as well as Independence, they appointed India's first Transgender principal in college also; they constructed separate toilets for them. They introduced SRS facilities in government hospitals because it can be a costly affair in private hospitals.
- *Sikkim* – In Sikkim, the state government provides Rupees 2000 monthly stipends to newborn Transgender babies and also provides education to these children.
- *Kerala* – Kerala government set up the justice board on 10th January 2017, exclusively for Transgender people. They are also providing legal aid services to ensure that these people will not

face discrimination and harassment. Kerala, in 2015, adopted a "State Policy for Transgender" that calls for a society where men, women and Transgender persons have equal access to capabilities, economic opportunities, assets and services, the right to dignity and freedom from violence and the right to expression. Reflecting the Transgender policy of the state, a daylong athletic meet was held on April 28, 2017. Kerala state literacy mission authority (KSLMA) was rolled out in SAMANWAYA, their main focus was on providing continuous education to members of the Transgender community.

Conclusion & Suggestions

Transgender persons face atrocities and discrimination throughout their life because of social stigma regarding gender and sexual orientation. The judiciary has taken a giant leap to help them achieve their fight for autonomy. The lack of awareness and implementation of NALSA judgment at the grassroots level are demerits of the spirit of decision. Specific legislation for the rights of Transgender person cannot conclude that their interests are meted out. The researchers Would like to suggest some reforms to curb and improve the status of Transgender-

- Sensitisation of police by organisations, seminars, workshops, and training programmes will help the community to access legal mechanisms.
- Every public authority and private entity must make rules for the representation of Transgender persons. If they are not adequately represented, how will any effective measures against discrimination be taken?
- Education curriculum must aware young children about gender equality, gender bias, and stereotypes. So that they can respect all gender in common parlance.
- Education Transgenders can reduce gender biases. Reservations in schools and colleges could result in progressive steps towards empowerment.
- No state can benefit its totality if its minorities are not backed up. Gender development plays a crucial role in the overall development of the country. The legislature shall make effective laws to ensure gender justice.

- This is the twenty-first century, an era of a globalised world where communities at large are connecting. Society must be Transformed to fight these rooted gender-based norms and stereotypes in our country.
- Statistical data is required to measure the direction of positive implementations. It would show the status of data on gender economic effect, crimes against Transgender, representation in schools and universities, income generation and overall development.
- Media and social networks have a broader and greater impact of social causes. Campaigns to promote gender equality and sensitisation would help create awareness among individuals at large.
- Establishes hotlines and helpline numbers to access help and support. They can keep the victim's identity a secret and provide counselling.
- Government must reach the local governments, village councils and NGOs to reach the grassroots level and give special instructions to respond and extend immediate help to any aggrieved Transgender persons.
- Awareness of schemes and fundamental rights of individuals' paramount rest will follow the procedure. So mass advertisements, campaigns, and special instructions must be spread at large. The identity of an individual should be treated with the utmost respect. The fight of the Transgender community is to be recognised as human and accepted into society. They wanted to be treated with the same respect and dignity as anyone in society. I think, as a society, we owe them that much.

References

Agarwal, S. (2020, December) *Transgenders to be included as a separate gender category in NCRB Reports: Centre informs Delhi high court*, Retrieved April 25, 2023, from https://www.livelaw.in/news-updates/Transgender-ncrbgender-category-delhi-high-court-karan-tripathi-166909?infinitescroll=1.

Agosto, S., Reitz, K., Ducheny, K., & Moaton, T. (2019). "Substance use and recovery in the Transgender and gender nonconforming (TGNC) older adult community." *Transgender and gender nonconforming health and aging*, 97-112.

Alliance, S. T. (2008). *Transgender experiences in Scotland.* Edinburgh: The Equality Network.

Andrews D., T.G. (2016). *A comparative study on the dimensions of victimisation among the resident and migrant Transgender persons of thoothukudi district tamilnadu.* https://shodhganga.inflibnet.ac.in:8443/jspui/handle/10603/175902

Annual Report (2015-2016). *Department of Health and Family Welfare, Ministry of Health and Family Welfare,* Government of India

Athreye, V. (2015). *The Life of Transgenders in India.* My India. Retrieved April 25, 2023, from https://www.mapsofindia.com/my-india/government/the-life-of-Transgenders

Babu, R. (2017, June 25). "In one week, eight Transgender employees quit working for Kochi metro." *Hindustan Times.* Retrieved April 25, 2023, from https://www.hindustantimes.com/india-news/in-one-week-eight-Transgender-employees-quit-working-for-kochi-metro/story-XDp6xgnA2Y6dhaAYcs8abP.html

Bianco, M. (2015, October 9). *Not having them at all: Why childfree women are banding together.* Quartz. Retrieved April 25, 2023, from https://qz.com/520484/not-having-them-at-all-why-childfree-women-are-banding-together

Census of India 2011, available at. https://www.census2011.co.in /Transgender.php

Chettiar, A. (2015). "Problems faced by Hijras (male to female Transgenders) in Mumbai with reference to their health and harassment by the police." *International Journal of Social Science and Humanity*, *5*(9), 752.

Datta, S. (2017). "We refuse to be subjects of experiment for those who do not understand us: Transgender persons' bill." *Economic and Political Weekly*, *52*(49).

Deccan Herald. (2020, March 13). *Bill seeking reservation for Transgenders in Parliament.* Retrieved April 25, 2023, from https://www.deccanherald.com/national/national-politics/bill-seeking-reservation-for-Transgenders-in-parliament-813443.html

Delvin, D. (2015, January 14). *Transvestites and cross-dressing.* Netdoctor. Retrieved April 25, 2023, from https://www.netdoctor.co.uk/healthy-living/sex-life/a2264/Transvestites-and-cross-dressing/

Divan, V., Cortez, C., Smelyanskaya, M., & Keatley, J. (2016). "Transgender social inclusion and equality: a pivotal path to development." *Journal of the International AIDS Society*, *19*, 20803.

Goel, I. (2018). "What Does it Mean to be a Hijra Mother?." *Economic and Political Weekly*, *53*(8).

Grant, J. M., Motter, L. A., & Tanis, J. (2011). "Injustice at every turn: A report of the national Transgender discrimination survey." Washington, DC: National Center for Transgender Equality and National Gay and Lesbian Task Force, 2011

Greenwald, R. (2023, January 28). *Is being a Transgender child traumatic?* Trauma Institute & Child Trauma Institute. Retrieved April 25, 2023, from https://www.ticti.org/blog/Trans/

Konduru, D., & Hangsing, C. (2018). "Socio–Cultural Exclusion and Inclusion of Transgenders in India." *International Journal of Social Sciences and Management*, 5(1), 10-17.

Konduru, D., & Hangsing, C. (2018). "Socio–cultural exclusion and inclusion of Trans genders in India." *International Journal of Social sciences and management*, *5*(1), 10-17.

Mandhani, A. (2018, April 10). *Centre amends rules to include Transgender option in PAN cards [Read notification]*. Supreme Court News, Latest India Legal News, Supreme Court Updates, High Courts Updates, Judgments, Law Firms News, Law School News, Latest Legal News. Retrieved April 25, 2023, from https://www.livelaw.in/centre-amends-rules-include-Transgender-option-pan-cards-read-notification/

Nagarajan, R. (2014, May 30). "First count of third gender in census: 4.9 lakh | India news – Times of India." *The Times of India.* Retrieved April 25, 2023, from https://timesofindia.indiatimes.com/india/first-count-of-third-gender-in-census-4-9-lakh/articleshow/35741613.cms

National Human Rights Commission. (2017). "Study on Human rights of Transgender as a Third Gender." *New Delhi: The National Human Rights Commission.[Google Scholar].*

Ng, S., Lakshmee, L., Singh, L. R., Singh, R. L., & Devi, N. P. (2018). "Relationship between socio-demographic factors and subjective well-being among Transgender in Manipur." *International Journal of Research in Economics and Social Sciences (IJRESS)*, *8*(1).

Ng, S., Lakshmee, L., Singh, L. R., Singh, R. L., & Devi, N. P. (2018). "Relationship between socio-demographic factors and subjective well-being among Transgender in Manipur." *International Journal of Research in Economics and Social Sciences (IJRESS)*, *8*(1).

Revathi, A. T. (2010). *The truth about me: A hijra life story.* Penguin UK.

Sawant, N. S. (2017). "Transgender: status in India." *Annals of Indian Psychiatry*, *1*(2), 59.

Shaikh, S., Mburu, G., Arumugam, V., Mattipalli, N., Aher, A., Mehta, S., & Robertson, J. (2016). "Empowering communities and strengthening systems to improve Transgender health: outcomes from the Pehchan programme in India." *Journal of the International AIDS Society*, *19*, 20809.

Sudha M. (2015). *Stigma and Quality of Life of Aravanis* (Ph.D. thesis). National Institute of Indian Council of Medical Research Chennai,. Retrieved from https://shodhganga.inflibnet.ac.in/jspui/bitstream/ 10603/173168/13.

The Times of India. (2016, April 17). *Police harass Transgenders most, says study | Chennai news – Times of India.* Retrieved April 25, 2023, from https://timesofindia.indiatimes.com/city/chennai/police-harass-Transgenders-most-says-study/articleshow/51869919.cms

Thilakavathi S, Ernest N, Narang A, Mehendale S. (2016). "Sexual Network, Sexual Practices and Sexual Health of Hijras and Other Trans-Women Populations in 17 States of India: A Qualitative Study." *International Journal of Health Sciences and Research*, ISSN: 2249-9571.

United Nations (2007). "Theoretical concepts of social exclusion." Chapter 1. In: *Literature review on social exclusion in the ESCWA region.* New York, NY: United Nations. Pp.2-7.

Veena KV. & Sridevi PL., S. (2011). "Social exclusion has a Negative Impact on the Health of Transgender." *Indian Streams Research Journal.* 1(6).

Venkatrama Raju, D., & Beena, K. S. (2015). "A study on socio-economic issues of third genders in Tamilnadu." *International Journal of Science and Research*, *4*(7), 1354-1357.

CHAPTER 17

Concerning Transgender People and their Legal Rights in the 21st Century

Prateek Singh

Transgender individuals are people whose identities do not conform to the conventional gender standards, which classify genders solely as male or female. Those conventions define genders only as male or female. They have been subjected to discrimination, social persecution, and even physical assault because their gender identity has not been accepted by society. Some socio-cultural groups of Transgender persons are known as Hijras, Jogappas, Sakhi, or Aradhis, for example. In addition, some individuals do not belong to any of these groups but are nonetheless referred to as Transgender people individually. This article discusses the rights of Transgender people in India, where it is recognised that Transgender people have the right to be protected by the law and have the right to be recognised as a third gender. Transgender took their rights from the Indian Constitution in the same way as the Constitution guaranteed justice and equality to all citizens of India. According to "India : Welfare Board for Transgenders." In 2021, in order to protect the rights of Transgender people, the government passed the Transgender Person (Protection of Rights) Act, 2019, which prohibits discrimination against Transgender in employment, education, and health services. In addition, the government has implemented welfare measures to ensure the safety of Transgender people.

Transgender Rights in India

People who identify as Transgender defy the notion that there are only two genders: men and women. Transgender people differ from their male and female counterparts in appearance, personal qualities, and behaviour. Transgender persons are exposed to social oppression since society does not recognise their gender identification. As a result, Transgender people suffer from the physical violence committed against them. Being different from the other gender makes Transgender people vulnerable to social oppression. The primary challenges they face throughout their lives include a lack of access to education, which can lead to unemployment and homelessness; a dearth of mental health services and medical facilities; depression and alcoholism; and prejudice. They have been granted rights by the Constitution of India. Also, the Supreme Court of India has given them the right to be recognised as the "Third Gender" and has granted them various welfare measures to defend their rights and resolve their concerns.

Acceptance as a Member of a Third Gender

People who identify as Transgender have historically been subjected to discrimination since their gender identity was not recognised in the eyes of the law or by society, and Transgender people were required to write male or female in place of their gender designation. In order to end the prejudice that Transgender people face and to better protect their legal rights, the Supreme Court of India declared that Transgender people belong to a third gender. The Court requested that the centre regard Transgender people as a socially and economically deprived class and provide them permission to get admission to educational institutions and jobs based on their third gender category. Additionally, the Court requested that the centre treat Transgender people like children. In the seminal decision of National Legal Service Authority v. Union of India, the Honourable Supreme Court of India has recognised them as the other genders like male and female. This decision was a watershed moment for the legal recognition of the third gender in the eyes of the law. Previously, the third gender had not been given legal recognition. Equal rights and protection are afforded to the Transgender individual by the Court under Articles 14, 15, 16, and 21. As the individual had a constitutional right to be recognised as either a man or a female, the Court emphasised the importance of the right to dignity and giving the respect it deserved for their gender identity, which was founded on newly assigned sex as a result of sex reassignment surgery.

In addition, the Court emphasised the importance of the right to dignity. Therefore, individuals who identify as Transgender are entitled to the protection of the law in all areas of governmental activity, including the fields of education and work. The supremacy of the rule of law in India ensures that everyone is treated equally in front of the law. Nevertheless, the Transgender community faces a never-ending uphill battle since members of this group must fight against oppression, abuse, and prejudice from every sector of society, including their own families and friends, as well as society as a whole. The lives of Transgender individuals are a constant struggle since they are not accepted everywhere and are shunned by society. This makes every day an uphill battle.

In contrast to this, the Supreme Court of India, in a landmark decision that was handed down by a division bench consisting of Justices K.S. Radhakrishnan and A.K. According to Agrawal (2016), in the case of National Legal Services Authority v. Union of India and Others, Sikri was the judge. The Writ Petition (Civil) No.400 of 2012(NALSA) acknowledged the existence of a third gender in addition to the male and female categories. Agarwal (2020) says, "Recognition of Transgenders as a third gender is not a social or medical issue but a human rights issue," Justice K.S. Radhakrishnan told the Supreme Court while handing down the ruling.

The right of equality before the law and equal protection of the law is guaranteed by Articles 14 and 21 of the Constitution, respectively. By recognising diverse gender identities, the Court has broken the dual gender structure of 'man' and 'woman' recognised by society. The ability to choose one's gender identification is a fundamental component of leading a life with dignity, which again falls under the purview of Article 21 of the Constitution.

Furthermore, they cannot be discriminated against on the ground of gender as it is a violation of Articles 14, 15, 16 and 21. The Court also protects one's gender expression invoked by Article 19 (1) (a), and it held that "no restriction can be imposed on the free expression of one's gender." The Court noted that a person would not realise his dignity if he is forced to mature in a gender to which he does not belong or cannot relate, which will again hinder his development. The Supreme Court has given specific directions for the protection of the rights of Transgender persons by including a third category in documents like election cards, passports, driving licences and ration cards, and for admission in educational institutions and hospitals. The

Supreme Court h It encompasses the rights to life, liberty, equality, dignity, and freedom to think and speak whatever one chooses. In National Legal Service Authority v. Union of India, the Supreme Court was concerned with the grievances and suffering of the Transgender Community, who sought a legal declaration of their gender identity rather than the identity of male/female assigned to them at birth. Their request was that non-recognition of their gender identification be considered a violation of Articles 14 and 21 of the Indian Constitution.

The Honourable Court interpreted the meaning of Article 14. It held that the article provides protection to 'any person' and that the term' person' in this context includes the Transgender person as well. As a result, they all have the same entitlement to the legal protection of the law in all spheres of state activity as any other citizen of this country. The Court also concluded that Articles 15 and 16 are not intended to be confined to the biological sex of male or female. However, instead, they were written with the intention of including those who identify as neither male nor female. In addition, the Court referred to Articles 19(1)(a) and 19(2) before coming to the conclusion that a Transgender person's personality can be represented through their behaviour and appearance and that this expression cannot be limited or forbidden. In conclusion, the judge cited Article 21 of the Constitution; Agarwal (2020) states, "Hijras/ Eunuchs have to be considered as the third gender, over and above binary gender under our constitution and the laws."

In its final judgment, the Supreme Court of India decided that Transgender people, in addition to a binary gender, should be considered as a "third gender" to guarantee their rights under Part III of the Constitution of India and the laws established by the parliament and State legislature. It was done to ensure that Transgender people are not discriminated against. In a separate ruling, the Court ordered the state government to recognise the plaintiffs in accordance with their third gender identification. The Honourable Supreme Court also directed the government to abolish societal stigma against Transgender people, as well as to promote specific health programmes and provide equal protection to Transgender people.

Rights Provided by the Constitution of India

Every person is guaranteed justice in the preamble to the Constitution, which defines justice as "social, economic, and political equality of status." The policy of the Indian state, which recognised only male and female sex in the past, has denied people of the third gender several rights that go along with being an Indian citizen. According to Agrawal (2016), these rights include the right to vote, the right to own property, the right to marry, the right to claim a formal identity through a passport, and more importantly, the right to education, employment, and health care. Articles 14, 15, 16 and 21 state that their fundamental rights, which have been violated, deprive them of their most fundamental rights. In the NALSA judgement from 2014, the rights of Transgender people were examined for the first time. In that ruling, the Supreme Court of India emphasised the need to preserve and maintain the rights of Transgenders in accordance with the values of the Indian Constitution that are outlined in Articles 14, 15, 16, and 21. However, even though Articles 14, 15, and 16 guarantee the right to equality for all Indian citizens and Article 21 guarantees the right to freedom for all Indian citizens, Transgender people are not afforded their fundamental rights to freedom and equality. Within the geographical boundaries of India, Equality before the law or Equal Protection before the law is the topic of discussion under Article 14. Article 14 unmistakably fits under the definition of "person," which encompasses both male and female individuals and those of a third gender; hence, Transgender people have the right to be protected by the law under the Indian Constitution in all areas of state action. Article 15, which deals with the prohibition of discrimination based on religion, race, caste, and sex, includes the third gender under its scope as being the citizens. It means they cannot be discriminated against based on religion, race, caste, and sex. They have the right to defend their gender expression, primarily represented in the clothes they wear, their actions, and their behaviours. This article widens the notion of sex, encompassing "Psychological Sex" and gender identity within its purview. Agarwal 2020). Article 16 deals with equality of opportunity in areas of public employment, and this article is used to broaden the definition of sex. They have the right to employment and equal opportunity and should not be discriminated against based on their sexual orientation. Transgender people who are citizens of India have the right to employment.

Article 21, which addresses the preservation of life and personal liberty, stipulates that no one may be deprived of their right to life or personal liberty unless it is done in accordance with the due process of the law. Transgender people have been denied the right to life and their autonomy for centuries. As citizens of India, Transgender people should have the same rights as everyone else when protecting their freedoms and rights. In addition, the Supreme Court has acknowledged the right to dignity by including the concept of gender identification in its interpretation of Article 21. The case known as Navtej Singh Johar v. the Union of India deals with the decriminalisation of Section 377 of the Indian Penal Code. According to the Global Freedom of Expression Columbia University (2018), the central issue of the case was the constitutional validity of Section 377, which stated that "voluntarily carnal intercourse against the order of nature with any man, woman or animal shall be with punished with imprisonment for life, or with imprisonment which may extend to ten years with a fine."

The petition was filed stating that Section 377 was unconstitutional. The petitioner, in this case, submitted the writ petition to have the right to sexuality, the right to sexual autonomy, and the freedom to select a sexual partner recognised as components of the right, which is protected by Article 21 of the Constitution of India. In the current case, the petitioner stated that Section 377 violated Article 14 because it was imprecise in that it did not define "carnal intercourse against the order of nature." No discernible distinction existed between natural and unnatural forms of consenting sexual activity. In other words, the petitioner claimed that Section 377 was unconstitutional. Section 377 further violated Article 15 because it discriminates based on the sex of a person's sexual partner. It further violated Article 19 because it denied the ability to express one's sexual identity. These violations constitute additional violations of the Convention on the Rights of the Child.

In the current case, the Honourable Supreme Court concluded that Section 377 should be decriminalised and reaffirmed that homosexuality is not an abnormality but rather a variant of sexuality. Both of these conclusions were reached simultaneously. The Court went on to rule that discrimination based on a person's sexual orientation violates their right to equality and privacy since a person's sexual orientation is an essential component of their self-identity.

The Court also ruled that withholding some rights violates their right to life, a fundamental right that cannot be denied.

Prohibition against Discrimination

Transgender persons have historically been subjected to discrimination in various contexts, including work, housing, healthcare, and education. The social stigma and isolation that they experience as a result of the lack of resources that were made available to Transgender individuals are the root causes of the prejudice that they are subjected to. The Transgender Person (Protection of Rights) Act 2019 includes a ban against discrimination, which most crucially encompasses vital areas like employment, education, and healthcare sectors, in order to preserve the rights of Transgender people and to shield them from discrimination. These goals are to safeguard the rights of Transgender people and to protect them from discrimination.

Education

The education of Transgender people is equally important as the education of people of other male or female genders; however, Because of the social stigma that Transgender persons experience, they lose interest in and concentration on their studies and begin to feel shunned and disgraced. Furthermore, Transgender students are frequently denied admission to educational institutions because these institutions do not recognise the gender identities of Transgender students. The education of Transgender people is equally important. The Transgender Person-Protection of Rights Act 2019 mandates that educational institutions that are supported or recognised by the government must offer equal access to education, recreational facilities, and sports for Transgender people without engaging in any discrimination. It was done to defend the rights of Transgender people.

Employment

Transgender individuals have been subjected to discrimination in the workplace as well as discrimination in employment affairs. They are subjected to discrimination, most commonly in invasions of privacy, being passed over for jobs, and harassment, ultimately resulting in unemployment and poverty. The Transgender Person Protection Act states that no government or private entities are allowed to discriminate against Transgenders in employment, including recruitment and promotions. Every establishment should appoint a complaint officer to handle complaints related to the Act. It is to prevent the discrimination that Transgender people have experienced.

The petitioner, in this case, had previously sought a position as a woman police constable in the case known as Nangai v. the Superintendent of Police. The examinations of applicants were overseen and carried out in Chennai by the Tamil Nadu Uniformed Services Recruitment Board. The petitioner's application was approved, and the Superintendent of Police gave her an employment order in the Karur district. She was put through a complete physical examination when she was in the process of going through her training at the Police Recruit School in Vellore. The chromosomal pattern and her genitalia led the investigation to conclude that she was of the "Transgender" gender. The outcome of the medical exam directly opposed the information found on her birth certificate, medical records, and educational credentials. In later years, The Superintendent ordered her to be fired from her position as a lady policeman. In order to uphold her rights as a Transgender person, the Honourable Court reversed the Superintendent of Police's contested order of termination from service. The Honourable Court upheld that the petitioner has the liberty to choose a different gender identity as a third gender in the future based on the medical declaration.

Care for the Sick

The term "health care services for the Transgender person" solely refers to the medical procedure involved in the Transition, but "health" refers to an entire condition of complete physical, mental, and social wellness. Healthcare services for Transgender people are not available. In addition, the term "health care" can apply to various main and additional health care services, such as job opportunities, housing, and social acceptance of Transgender persons. Because Transgender people have historically faced significant health inequalities and barriers to accessing adequate healthcare treatments, they are more likely to experience mental health issues such as depression and attempted suicide, as well as physical and verbal abuse and even HIV. According to the Transgender Person (Protection of Rights) Act of 2019, the government should take appropriate actions to provide healthcare facilities to a Transgender persons, including separate HIV surveillance centres and sex reassignment surgeries, and

Transgender persons should be provided with comprehensive medical insurance plans. This is to safeguard them and assist them in living a happy life.

Welfare Measures

For a long period of time, Transgender people have been subjected to discrimination and neglect from society. However, in order to bring them back into the mainstream of society, several welfare measures have been taken for the Transgender person. For example, the land was supplied for Aravanis in Tamil Nadu. At the same time, the state government of Andhra Pradesh directed the Minority Welfare Department to identify "Hijras" as a minority group and to implement assistance packages for Transgender persons. In order to address the social welfare concerns of Transgender people, the Department of social welfare board in the Indian state of Tamil Nadu formed the 'Aravanigal/Transgender Women Welfare Board. According to the Transgender Person Protection Act 2019, the relevant government shall make efforts to guarantee the full participation of Transgender people in society and develop specific welfare programmes and measures to safeguard the rights of Transgender people. This provision was included in the Act.

Human Rights have been violated

They are denied the ability to participate in social and cultural activities, so their access to education, health care, and public spaces is restricted. This further deprives them of the constitutional guarantee of equality before the law and equal protection under the law (Sirohi, 2014). It has also been observed that the community faces discrimination as a result of the fact that they are not given the right to contest elections, right to vote (Article 326), employment, get licenses, etc., and as a result, they are treated as outcasts and untouchable. Because the Transgender community faces stigma and discrimination, it has fewer opportunities when compared to other communities. They are neither accepted by society nor given a chance to acquire an adequate education because of who they are. Thus, they do not go to school. Even though they are enrolled in a school, they are subjected to harassment and are tormented on a daily basis. As a result, they are either asked to leave the school or leave on their own. As a result of this, they resort to beggary and labour in the sex trade. Due to the practice of restricting job opportunities to either males or women, it is extremely rare for talented members of this society to find paid employment outside of the informal sector. They are pushed into sex work, which puts them at the highest risk of catching HIV as they consent to unprotected sexual intercourse because they fear rejection or they want to validate their gender via sex. Even if they do, they are mocked and ostracised, and as a result, they are forced to abandon their occupations. They are forced to engage in sex work, which puts them at great risk of obtaining HIV. Within the context of society, we refer to them as “vectors” of HIV. Other sexually Transmitted illnesses, such as rectal gonorrhoea, syphilis, and rectal Chlamydia, among others, increase a person’s likelihood of contracting HIV.

The Immoral Traffic Prevention Act of 1956, which was revised in 1986, is now a law that does not discriminate based on gender. The Act’s remit now encompasses both male and female sex workers, individuals whose gender identification was unclear and those who worked in the adult entertainment industry. Because of the legislation, both male and hijra sex workers are now considered criminal subjects. It provides the legal foundation for the police to arrest and intimidate Transgender sex workers. Same-sex relationships between consenting adults are considered illegal under section 377 of the IPC. This rule, which dates back to the colonial era, leaves members of the Transgender community open to harassment, extortion, and assault at the hands of the authorities. Pandian, a Transgender person, was taken into custody by the police and charged with stealing in the case of Jayalakshmi v. State of Tamil Nadu (Agrawal, 2016). At the police station, he was the victim of a sexual assault, which finally drove him to set himself on fire.

Case studies

The trauma that Laxmi Narayan Tripathy, a Hijra, experienced as a youngster may be expressed as follows: “I felt different from the boys of my age (as I was born as a boy) and was feminine in the ways that I carried myself.” Because of her femininity, I was subjected to multiple instances of sexual harassment, sexual assault, and sexual abuse at a young age, and this occurred both inside and outside of the family. During the time that I was trying to come to grips with who I was, I was ostracised because of my uniqueness. I had no one to talk to, and I couldn’t share my emotions with anybody else. I was regularly called a ‘chakka’ and a ‘hijra’ by everyone. Later on, she associated with other Hijras and felt at home for the very first time in her life when she joined the Hijra community in Mumbai. This was the first time in her life that she felt at home.

A eunuch by the name of Siddarth Narrain has quite similar sentiments. He explains his perspective by saying, "When I was in the tenth standard, I came to the conclusion that the only way for me to feel at ease was to become a member of the Hijra community." My family learned at that time that I had frequent interactions with hijras, who were based in the city where we all lived. One day, while my dad was out of the house, my older brother began to beat me with a cricket bat, and my mum encouraged him to do it. In order to protect myself from the beatings, I locked myself in a room. After that, my mother and brother made an attempt to force their way into the room so they could continue beating me. Several of my cousins and aunts, and uncles got involved and got me out of the room.

A Transgender woman from Madurai named Madhu, who is 22 years old and whose name has been altered, explains why she no longer gets tested for the illness. She reveals, "I do not have the courage anymore. What will I do if they tell me that I have HIV or AIDS? Where am I going to go? How exactly will I educate myself? If I ever get tested positive for HIV, I really hope it kills me. Other people within the Transgender community have reported having life experiences that are comparable to their own. Because of their susceptibilities, they are forced to make concessions with regard to their health and safety. Messages to be delivered to the federal and state governments The Court has given the national and state governments many directives, which are as follows: In order to protect the fundamental rights of hijras and eunuchs, they ought to be given the same consideration as members of a third gender.

Recognise the necessity for the person to determine his or her gender and create a socially and educationally disadvantaged segment of persons eligible for reservations in public education and work settings. Making particular preparations for HIV sero-surveillance for Transgender people and providing adequate health facilities are also required. Deal with issues such as fear, gender dysphoria, shame, sadness, suicidal inclinations, and the like that they are dealing with. In order to ensure that Transgender persons have access to appropriate medical treatment in hospitals, steps such as creating separate wards and providing separate public restrooms should be adopted. Develop programmes of social welfare that will contribute to their overall growth. To increase general public awareness to give Transgender people the impression that they are an integral part of society and should not be ignored or mistreated in any way. By reframing the issues of the Transgender community as a question of rights, the judgment has marked a shift from the typically paternalistic and philanthropic stance of the state towards the Transgender population.

2014 Legislation titled the Right of Transgender Persons Bill

On December 12, 2014, the Bill was presented for consideration in *Rajya Sabha*, and on April 24, 2015, it was overwhelmingly approved with backing from all political parties. Tiruchi Siva, a representative for Tamil Nadu in the Indian Parliament, was the one who proposed this private member's Bill. Finally, the Bill in the *Rajya Sabha*, April 24th, is now observed as Transgender Day. The majority of the rights guaranteed by the Bill are fundamental freedoms, including the right to free speech, the right to life and personal liberty, the right to live in a community, and integrity, in addition to safeguards against torture, cruelty, and abuse, assault, and exploitation. There is a distinct article in the Bill that addresses Transgender children. The Bill also addresses education, work, social security, and health care issues. The chapter on employment contains two separate clauses that deal with the government's creation of plans for vocational training and self-employment of Transgender people.

The education chapter requires the government to provide Transgender pupils with inclusive education as well as adult education. There is a distinct provision that prohibits discrimination against those who identify as Transgender in any place, whether it be public or private. The government is asked to enhance social security and health care services through free SR's clinics and separate HIV clinics in the social security and health chapter. They should have the right to leisure activities, cultural experiences, and recreational opportunities. The government is in charge of ensuring that fundamental rights are upheld, including access to sanitary facilities and clean drinking water. The proposed legislation envisions establishing various commissions and agencies, including national and state commissions for Transgender people. The majority of the work that the Commission will be doing will be in the form of inquiries or recommendations about anomalies in applying the law or abuses of the rights of Transgender people. The Commissions have the authority to issue summonses to witnesses, collect evidence, and perform other legal functions. Hate speech directed towards Transgender individuals can result in a sentence of incarceration for up to a year if proven intentional.

References

Agrawal, S. (2016). "Transgender Community – They Are Neither A Sin, Nor A Choice: An Analysis." *Indian Social Science Journal*, 5(1), 47.

"India : Welfare Board for Transgenders." 2021. MENA Report, December.

Anmol K. (2023). *Rights of Transgender under the Indian legal system.* Legal Service India – Law, Lawyers and Legal Resources. Retrieved April 25, 2023, from https://www.legalserviceindia.com/legal/article-6958-rights-of-Transgender-under-the-indian-legal-system.html

ILO. (2022). *Rights of Transgenders in India.* Law Firm in India: India Law Offices LLP – Pan India. Retrieved April 25, 2023, from https://www.indialawoffices.com/legal-articles/rights-of-Transgenders-in-india

India Code. (2019). *India code: Transgender persons (Protection of rights) Act, 2019.* Retrieved April 25, 2023, from https://www.indiacode.nic.in/handle/123456789/13091?sam_handle=123456789/1362

Rural India. (2019). *The Transgender persons (Protection of rights) Act, 2019.* People's Archive of Rural India. Retrieved April 25, 2023, from https://ruralindiaonline.org/en/library/resource/the-Transgender-persons-protection-of-rights-act-2019/

Solanki, A. S., & Desai, N. (n.d.). *India's new law on the protection of rights of Transgender persons.* International Bar Association | International Bar Association. Retrieved April 25, 2023, from https://www.ibanet.org/article/0F3AE21B-0170-4BF7-95DD-45B07EF1CAF6

Sirohi, S. (2014, July 1). *Recognition of third gender is truly landmark.* Alive, 381, 44.

Subramanian, S. (2018, September 6). *India's historic gay-rights ruling and the slow march of progress.* The New Yorker. Retrieved April 25, 2023, from https://www.newyorker.com/news/news-desk/indias-historic-gay-rights-ruling-and-the-slow-march-of-progress

Global Freedom of Expression Columbia University. (2018, November 27). *Navtej Singh Johar v. Union of India.* Global Freedom of Expression. Retrieved April 25, 2023, from https://globalfreedomofexpression.columbia.edu/cases/navtej-singh-johar-v-union-india/

Global Freedom of Expression. (2020, April 16). *National legal services authority v. Union of India.* Retrieved April 25, 2023, from https://globalfreedomofexpression.columbia.edu/cases/national-legal-services-authority-v-union-of-india/

Agarwal, S. (2020, August 14). *What are the rights of Transgender in India.* iPleaders. Retrieved April 25, 2023, from https://blog.ipleaders.in/legal-rights-of-Transgender-india/

Singh, A. (2021, September 2). *Right to equality under the Indian constitution.* iPleaders. Retrieved April 25, 2023, from https://blog.ipleaders.in/right-to-equality/

Authors

1. **Aditi Dubey** is a student of BA LLB (Honours) at the School of Law in Christ (Deemed to be University), Lavasa campus, Pune – 412112, Maharashtra State, India. Email: aditidd2004@gmail.com

2. **Akash Devangan** is a Senior Research Fellow at Jawaharlal Nehru University, Delhi, pursuing his PhD, and is an alumnus of the Indian Institute of Mass Communication (IIMC), New Delhi. With a good blend of work experience in media and media academics, he has authored several research papers and worked in various National Media Houses. Email: akash97034@gmail.com

3. **Ajeet Kumar Jogi** is a doctoral candidate doing research in the Department of Anthropology, School of Social Sciences at Hyderabad Central University Telangana, India. His research area includes tribal studies, state policy and tribal livelihood, socio-cultural anthropology, globalisation and tribal economy. He has a recipient of national fellowship UGC New Delhi. He has presented a paper on "State Policy over the Forest, Land and Livelihood and Survivals of Indigenous Communities in India: Problem and Prospects" at the Royal Anthropological Institute of London, UK. He can be contacted on ajeetjjogi.hcu@gmail.com

4. **Anju Harbansh** is a doctoral candidate doing research at HNLU Naya Raipur, Chattisgarh, India. She can be contacted on anjuharbansh@gmail.com

5. **Anya Gonsalves** is a BA LLB (Honours), School of Law, Christ (Deemed to be University), Lavasa campus, Pune – 412112, Maharashtra State, India, anyagonsalves@gmail.com

6. **Dr. Santosh Kumar** works as Associate Professor and Head of the Department of Journalism & Mass Communication at Shri Rawatpura Sarkar University, Raipur, Chhattisgarh. He completed his PhD & M.Phil from the Centre for Diaspora Studies at the Central University of Gujarat, Gandhinagar (Gujarat), India, on Diasporic Communication. He got the ICSSR Travel Grant

Fellowship for Data Collection Abroad UK. He qualified for the UGC NET in 2018. He has convened ICSSR Sponsored Two-Day National Seminar On "Transgender, Society and Media" on 20-21 March 2023, also did Three Day National Seminar on Diverse Dimensions of Indigenous Language and Culture, 'Tribal Society: Present Status & Future Directions' on October 28 – 30, 2021. His research area of interest includes Human Communication, Journalism and Society, Film Critical Theory, Human Migration and Diaspora Studies, Transnationalism, Multiculturalism, and Human Inequalities. He has recently edited the books: (1) *Diaspora, Emigration and Inequality: A Survey in World Forum (2023), (2) Transgender, Society and Media (2023)* Email: santoshcug@gmail.com

7. **Firdaus Shahnaz** is a PhD Research Scholar, Department of English, Vinoba Bhave University, Hazaribag Jharkhand, India. Contact No.: 7991174827 Email Id: firdausshahnaz1@gmail.com

8. **Khushboo Sahu**, pursuing a Ph.D. at the Department of Social Work from Guru Ghasidas Vishwavidhyalaya, Koni Bilaspur CG., possess a post-graduation in social work background. She is keenly interested in social service from underrated and underprivileged communities like third-gender and widows. She has taken the thesis topic of the third gender about their social exclusion and educational rights. She can be reached on khushboosahu1912@gmail.com

9. **Manisha Bose** is working as an Assistant Professor at the Department of Social Work at Shri Rawatpura Sarkar University, Raipur, Chhattisgarh-492015.

10. **Ms. Aditi Mishra**, BA LLB (Honours), School of Law, Christ (Deemed to be University), Lavasa campus, Pune – 412112, Maharashtra State, India. Email: aditiarer0@gmail.com

11. **Ms. Avilasha Sarkar**, BA LLB (Honours), School of Law, Christ (Deemed to be University), Lavasa campus, Pune – 412112, Maharashtra State, India. Email: avilashasarkar13@gmail.com

12. **Ms. Rhea Eleanor Rhine**, BA LLB (Honours), School of Law, Christ (Deemed to be University), Lavasa campus, Pune – 412112, Maharashtra State, India, Email: rhearhine13@gmail.com

13. **Nikita Nimbalkar** is working as an Assistant Professor at the Department of Economics at Fergusson College, Pune, India. She could be contacted via nikita.nimbalkar@fergusson.edu.

14. **Prateek Singh** is a BA LLB (Honours) student at the School of Law, Christ (Deemed to be University), Lavasa Campus, Pune, Maharashtra-412112, India. Email: s.prateek2412@gmail.com

15. **Rudra Bhanu Pratap Singh** is a Research Scholar at the Department of Journalism & Mass Communication at Shri Rawatpura Sarkar University, Raipur, Chhattisgarh-492015. His research area implies media studies, film studies, film and advertisement production. He could be contacted via rudra4movie@gmail.com.

16. **Satyabrata Sahoo** is a Master student in IGNOU, New Delhi pursuing MA Folklore & Culture Studies, School of Interdisciplinary and Transdisciplinary studies. He is an independent Researcher, conducting studies on post-Human studies, Transhuman Anthropology, Ludological Narratives, studying bodies & its discourses, LGBTIQA+ Studies. Anyone can connect with the author on his e-mail: satyabitu123@outlook.com

17. **Soumik Bose** is a Research Scholar at the Department of Mechanical Engineering at the National Institute of Technology, Raipur, Chhattisgarh – 492010.

18. **Swakshadip Sarkar** is a PhD student at Te Herenga Waka – Victoria University of Wellington. They have been involved in activism both in India and the UK where they have participated in several outreach programs to raise awareness about the issues faced by LGBTQ+ individuals. They are personally interested in LGBTQ+ activism and research, especially in the broader area of gender equality and intersectionality. Anyone can connect with the author on his e-mail: swakshadip.sarkar@vuw.ac.nz

19. **Vijaya is a Doctoral** Candidate doing research at Bhaskar Institute of Journalism and Mass Communication, Bundelkhand University, Jhansi, Uttar Pradesh-284128. Her area of research includes Family Communication, Human Communication, Child and Parent communication, Indian Journalism and Mass Communication in India, etc.

20. **Yogesh Vaishnaw** is an Assistant Professor at Amity University Chhattisgarh and a reputed media professional in Central India. He has received several awards, journalism fellowship and recognitions throughout his academic & media career, including two gold medals for outstanding academic performance. He is an alumnus of Makhanlal Chaturvedi National University of Journalism & Communication Bhopal, Kushabhau Thakre Journalism University Raipur & Central University of Chhattisgarh. Email: yogivaishnav91191@gmail.com

Index